Rev. Jean Berthier, M.S.
(1840-1908)

The Writer

By

Rev. Victor Hostachy, M.S.
Translated by Fr. Joseph Boutin, M.S.

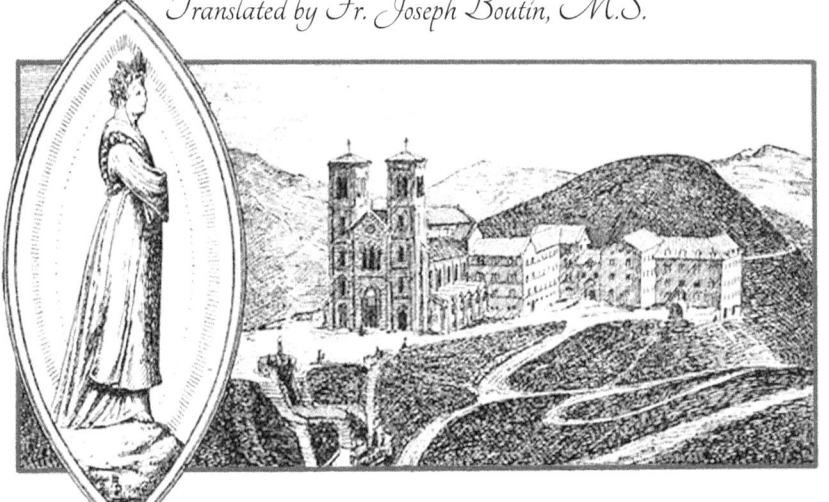

Second Edition, 2018
Expanded and updated

Missionaries of La Salette Corporation
915 Maple Avenue
Hartford, CT 06114-2330, USA
web site: www.lasalette.org

First Edition: 1943 Le R. P Jean Berthier, 1840-1908 L'écrivain, part three of Figures Missionnaires.

Unpublished Edition: Translated to English in 1953 by Fr. Joseph Boutin, M.S.

Second Edition: Expanded and updated revision to the English Translation of 1953.

Imprimi Potest:

Very Rev. Fr. Rene Butler, M.S., Provincial Superior, Missionaries of Our Lady of La Salette, Province of Mary, Mother of the Americas, 915 Maple Avenue, Hartford, CT 06114-2330 USA

Copyright @ Feast of Our Lady of La Salette, September 19, 2018, Missionaries of Our Lady of La Salette, Province of Mary, Mother of the Americas

All rights reserved. No part of this book may be reproduced, stored in a retrieval system, or transmitted, in any form or by any means, electronic, mechanical, photocopying, recording or otherwise, without the written permission of La Salette Communications Center Publications, 947 Park Street, Attleboro, MA 02703

Printed in the United States of America

Booklet Design and Digital Formatting: Jack Battersby and Fr. Ron Gagne, M.S.

Editor: Fr. Ron Gagne, M.S.

This and other La Salette titles available in E-book format at www.lasalette.org

IBSN: 978-1-946956-19-4

Contents

Letter of Reverend Father J. M. Fournel— i

Foreword— iii

Bibliography— vii

Chronological list of Fr. Berthier's Written Works— ix

1 Early Years— 1

2 First Contacts with La Salette— 10

3 At Grenoble and the Chartreuse— 20

4 In the Service of Our Lady and Her People— 28

5 Foundation of a School for Missionaries— 43

6 First Threats of Anticlericalism— 58

7 The Popular Writings of Fr. Berthier— 72

8 Promotion of Fr. Berthier's Books— 85

9 His Project of "Late Vocations"— 101

10 His New Foundation – A Sequel to La Salette — 116

Epilog— 134

Letter of Reverend Father J. M. Fournel

Provincial of the Missionaries of the Holy Family

J.M.J., Manissy, January 10, 1942

Dear Reverend Father,

You requested as a preface to your excellent book on Very Reverend Jean Berthier, the Founder of our Institute, a letter from Very Reverend Father Trampe, Superior General of the Missionaries of the Holy Family, or in case the latter was unable to send one, something from the erudite Father Ramers. Both would have been most happy to accede to your wishes and would have done this most competently: Fr. Trampe, because he lived many years with Fr. Berthier and was a member of his council; Fr. Ramers because of the thorough researches he made everywhere our venerable founder spent some time or lived.

Since, owing to circumstances, neither one could be contacted, you called on my services and asked me to write a few lines by way of a preface. Notwithstanding my surprise at such a great honor, I will attempt to set down what my heart dictates.

First of all, allow me to tell you that reading your book will be its best recommendation to the public. As they peruse its pages, those who were acquainted with Fr. Berthier will feel as if they are in actual contact with him and those who were not fortunate enough to have known him will be most edified. And thus it is, dear Father, that you have painted a splendid picture of your hero and have presented in its true light this apostolic soul, so overflowing with zeal and charity.

You have ably depicted the deep love of God which inflamed his soul and his tender devotion to Our Lady of La Salette, one which he passed on to his children along with the devotion to the Holy Family. These are the two powerful forces which set in motion the great projects he did not hesitate to undertake for the glory of God and the salvation of souls.

He always considered himself as the mouthpiece of the Virgin in tears and looked upon the touching words: "Well, my children, you will make this known to all my people" as addressed directly to himself. He was so earnest about his role of apostle that the salvation of souls was practically an obsession with him, with the result that in order to cooperate in this work, he made use of every means possible, becoming at one and the same time, missionary, writer, professor and founder.

You have made it a point to stress his talent as a writer; I congratulate you on that. Fr. Berthier was indeed a real writer, if not a great one, at least a prolific one. That is exactly what he wanted to be. He did not seek honors; what consumed him was zeal for souls. He became a writer because he was an apostle. You have expressed that with much grace and unction and every reader, as he peruses your book, will easily detect the veneration and affection you have for your illustrious confrere. Such delicacy and sincerity on your part can but result in binding more closely the ties which unite our religious community with yours.

Fr. Berthier enfolded both these families in the one and same love; he became the founder of one and chose to remain a member of the other until death. What a joy and what a comfort to know that from heaven above he is watching over both of them!

May the Holy Family of Nazareth and Our Lady of La Salette, both so highly glorified by Fr. Berthier, bless your book and give it all the success it deserves! May it produce much holiness in souls, nurture holy vocations for the cause of God and may it give rise to noble emulation in the cause of the Christian Apostolate and Catholic Action. With these wishes, I remain your brother in our Lord.

January 10, 1943, Feast of the Holy Family.

J. M. Fournel, M.S.F.
Prov. Superior

Foreword

Fr. Jean Berthier, M.S.

Fr. Archier and Fr. Giraud found the driving force of their missionary lives in the apparition of Our Lady of La Salette; the words spoken by the Virgin inspired the former to become a Missionary of "Action"; meditation on the meaning of Mary's tears made out of the latter a man of "contemplation".

Through his profound humility, Fr. Archier was able to erect a sanctuary to the glory of this Virgin and assist in laying the foundations of an institute dedicated to her tears and her apostolate; as a result of much suffering, Fr. Giraud was able to sow in abundance the seeds of a life of victim and sacrifice in the souls of those who wished to follow in the footsteps of the Weeping Virgin.

A third great missionary now comes on the scene, one who combines in himself the "action" of the one and the "contemplation" of the other. Fr. Berthier reproduced in his life as an enterprising and devoted missionary their ideas, their ideals and their zeal. He rather favors Fr. Archier since he has a marked preference for action.

He does not imitate them in a haphazard way, neither does he copy them slavishly; he follows after his own fashion in the footsteps of these two with whom he lived many years, yet he is original, independent, sure of himself and equally as successful in the Salettine Apostolate. He will spread the name of La Salette much further than they did because of his many widely read books and his most active apostolate made him better known than they were.

He served his community well even though he never held the reins of high command as did Fr. Archier; he founded an institute very similar to his own.

His mysticism was not as profound as that of Fr. Giraud yet it reached far more souls and he did much more than the latter to spread the Salettine idea of restoring Christian society back to God.

The Virgin of La Salette wanted her supernatural message made known throughout the world; Fr. Jean Berthier, through Mary's help, did his utmost to reach the entire Christian world and restore it to Christ; this he did by means of his easily understood and popular spiritual writings and his apostolic zeal.

Fr. Giraud on the other hand wrote for a select group and his scope was limited to religious and priestly souls; Fr. Berthier, without neglecting this field of the apostolate, wrote for the six-year-old child and the mature theologian, the virgin dedicated to God and the mother of a family, the seminarian and the young girl. When he had exhausted all these categories, he wrote the most successful of his books: *The Book for All* (*Le Livre de Tous*).

His genius came into contact with more souls than did that of Fr. Giraud. It took in every class of society, each family of these different groups as well as the individual members of the family. His life and his books were the strong forces of propaganda which he used to lead everyone to Christ and to love for Christ.

He is the equal of Fr. Giraud both in his rare ability at imparting knowledge effectively and in his deep spiritual insight. He treats all subjects with great ease and shows a rare facility in assimilating the thoughts of others. He is by no means narrow-minded; we do not find in him that originality which would characterize some special teaching as distinctively his own, but he did know how to set forth in a new light and thoroughly explain many points of Christian doctrine in exact and clear language.

He came into contact with personalities of all types and dedicated himself to every phase of the priestly ministry; he fearlessly undertook material and spiritual projects; at other times he busied himself with duties apparently opposed to each other, yet all of these he coordinated and directed towards his one great objective which was to restore the Blessed Virgin and her Son, Christ, to their rightful place in Christian society and in the souls of everyone.

Fr. Giraud is the priest-victim type and contemplative whereas Fr. Berthier is the model priest-missionary, the good pastor and converter.

Fr. Victor Hostachy, M.S. (1885-1967), noted author and historian

Fr. Giraud received his mandate of a high spiritual life at La Salette, at the feet of the Virgin who suffers and offers herself up in sacrifice to the divine justice along with the victim of Calvary; on the other hand, Fr. Berthier received his mission from the Virgin Apostle who speaks to all her people, who outlines a minimum program of Christian spirituality, gives it to the two shepherds of the mountain with a specific command to make it known everywhere, at all times, to make it bear fruit in average souls as well as in souls of high spirituality: *Well, my children, you will make this known to all my people.*

Briefly then, Fr. Giraud is the Virgin weeping; Fr. Berthier, the Virgin speaking.

Fr. Berthier wrote the following at the end of his book, *The Wonders of La Salette*:

"In the Apparition of La Salette there is found not only reparation but zeal also. Of old we have seen the ancient Fathers of the desert who led there a most recollected life apart from the world, leave their solitude when the church was in peril and give themselves over to the saving of souls who were in danger of falling into heresy. The Virgin of La Salette, as it were, leaves heaven in order to exhort souls to return to God; yet, while exhorting her children to prayer and penance, she twice repeats the following words: 'Well, my children, you will make this known to all my people' ".

"She wants action as well as reparation; action that will promote the glory of God by putting an end to sin everywhere, in our families, in our neighborhoods, in every place we can exert our influence; action that will be a source of good in others through our compassion over their weakness and misfortunes, through our sympathy and kindness towards them, all of which will later on allow us to reprimand them in all sweetness and exhort them to conversion". (1)

This program of Our Lady of La Salette was the ideal that motivated the life, the writings and the actions of Fr. Berthier, the perfect missionary of Mary's tears and teachings, a man trained by Frs. Archier and Giraud and later on as their beloved and devoted collaborator.

Endnote

(1) *The Wonders of La Salette* by Fr. Jean Berthier, M.S., Paris, Tequi (1898).

Bibliography

Articles by Fr. Charles Grenat, M.S., in the *"Bulletin des oeuvres des Missionaires de La Salette"*, March and July 1909: May and July 1910. Necrology: Rev. Jean Berthier, Missionary of La Salette.

An Apostle, of our days or ***The Life and Spirit of Very Reverend Jean Berthier, Missionary of La Salette, Founder of the Missionaries of the Holy Family, (1840-1908)*** by Rev. J. M. De Lombaerde, Missionary of the Holy Family (1910), Institute of the Holy Family, Grave, (Holland).

Rev. Fr. Peter Joseph Ramers, M.S.F. of the same institute of the Holy Family, wrote an interesting thesis on his founder which he submitted for his doctorate at the University of Fribourg (Switzerland). It is the result of much research and very well documented. We refer you to the manuscript of this thesis which was graciously loaned us even before it was officially submitted or appeared in book form. We made good use of this and the summary thereof which the author wrote in *The Holy Family Review*, a magazine published in six languages: French, German, Dutch, Polish, English and Portuguese. We commend Fr. Ramers very highly and we give him due credit for placing Fr. Berthier in his proper historical setting and milieu as well as for the sound, clear and erudite review he made of his written work.

Antoine Bossan – *Notes* on the origin of the community of the Missionaries of La Salette, from 1862 to 1864.

Joseph Perrin: *Pilgrimage Notes (1864-1871).*

Archives of the Institute of the Missionaries of La Salette:

- *Register of professions.*
- *Annals of the Residence of Loech in Valais,* (1881-1899).

Archives of the Institute of the Holy Family:

- Fr. Berthier's letters to Fr. Douare.

- Letters of Cardinal Langenieux.
- Large correspondence of Fr. Berthier and various manuscripts.

Annals of Our Lady of La Salette (*Annales de Notre-Dame de La Salette*)

- *Bulletin of the Works of the Missionaries of La Salette.*
- *The Holy Family Review.*

Translator, Fr. Joseph Boutin M. S. 1902-1986

Chronological list of Fr. Berthier's Written Works

1868: *The Mother According to the Mind of God or Duties of the Christian Mother Towards Her Children*, over 500 pages.

1866: *Brief Recital of the Apparition of Our Lady of La Salette*, 16 pages.

1868: *Youth and the Christian Virgin at the School of the Saints*, 502 pages.

1871: *Our Lady of La Salette, Her Apparition, Her Cult*, Historical Notes, 80 pages.

1872: *Novena in Honor of Our Lady of La Salette*, which also includes "Historical notes on the Apparition and Cult of Our Lady of La Salette", 160 pages.

1872: *Sententiae et exempla biblica e veteri et novo testamento, excepta et ordinata ad usum concionatorum, moderatorumque animarum et praesertim juniorum clericorum, semnariorumque alumnorum* (Decisions and biblical examples from the Old and New Testament, except for the use of the array vendors, moderatorumque souls, and especially for the young clerks, students and seminarians), 400 pages.

1874: *On the States of the Christian Life and Vocation*, 306 pages.

1877: *Pilgrimage of Our Lady of La Salette or Guide of the Pilgrim on the Holy Mountain*, – in collaboration with Fr. Joseph Perrin, M.S. 114 pages.

1878: *What is My Vocation and What Advice Should I Give on the Choice of a State of Life?* 102 pages.

1880: *Easy Method to Prepare Small Children for the Sacrament of Penance*, 36 pages.

1883: *The Priest in the Ministry of Preaching, of the Missions and of Re-

treats, 600 pages.

1883: *The Faithful and Religious Soul Enlightened on the Truths of Faith and the Duties of the Christian and Perfect Life*, 420 pages.

1883: *The Work of Vocations to La Salette*, 130 pages.

1887: *Breve Compendium Theologiae Dogmaticae et Moralis (A brief Compendium of Dogmatic and Moral Theology)*, 615 pages.

1888: *The Book for All*, 367 pages.

1888: *The Virgin Mary, Devotion to Her, Her Cult, or Theological Catechism on the Blessed Virgin*, 120 pages.

1888: *Our Lord Jesus Christ – What We Owe Him*, 150 pages.

1891: *Method for Assisting the Dying*, 16 pages.

1892: *Summary of Dogmatic and Moral Theology*, 840 pages.

1892:

- *A bouquet of Most Beautiful Flowers*, 160 pages.
- *A Basket of Most Beautiful Flowers*, 160 pages.
- *A Garland of Most Beautiful Flowers*, 160 pages.

1892: *Most Remarkable Historical Words and Incidents*, 756 pages.

1893: *The Religious State, its Excellence, Advantages, Obligations and Privileges*, 456 pages.

1893: *A Book for Little Children*, 207 pages.

1894: *The Priesthood, its Excellence, Obligations, Rights, Advantages and Privileges*, 852 pages.

1895: *Examination of Conscience and a Method for Prayer*, 22 pages.

1896: *Man As He Should Be*, 543 pages.

1896: *The Young Man As He Should Be*, 497 pages.

1898: *The Marvels of La Salette*, 352 pages.

1901: *The Work of the Holy Family of Late Vocations for the Missions*, 61 pages.

1902: *Blessed are the Pure of Heart or Perfect Chastity*, 368 pages.

1904: *The Art of Being Happy*, 465 pages.

1904: *The Key of Heaven*, 339 pages.

1907: *The Cult and Imitation of the Holy Family*, 485 pages.

> **V. HOSTACHY**
> Missionnaire de Notre-Dame de La Salette
>
> FIGURES MISSIONNAIRES
>
> III
>
> # Le R. P. Jean BERTHIER
>
> (1840-1908)
>
> ## L'écrivain
>
>
>
> Editions de la Revue « LES ALPES »
> 1, Rue Villars. GRENOBLE
>
> 1943

Title page of the original French version of this book

1
Early Years

Father Berthier was born February 24, 1840, at Chatonnay, a little commune in Isère, located half-way between Grenoble and Vienne. The baptismal records of his church have him registered as John-Baptist. He will usually be called John Peter. He preferred John for short and considered Saint John the Evangelist as his patron saint and, like him, he wanted to be an apostle both by word and pen.

Fr. Berthier's home town of Chantonnay, France

When he was six years old – the year of the apparition of the Blessed Virgin at La Salette, in 1846 – he had already become the little missionary as it was then his custom to preach to his little playmates and deliver fervent exhortations to them. (1)

When he was twelve –the year of his First Communion and that in which the Institute of the Missionaries of La Salette was founded, in 1852 – he was even then recruiting vocations for the Lord and carefully cultivating his own.

His parents, respectable farmers, had a large farm located on the outskirts of the village, on a road leading to the hillock called "Calvary" because a way of the cross had been erected there.

His mother, Marie Putoud, will serve as the model later on and will be described in his book, *The Mother according to the Mind of God*. He used often to say: "The greatest grace that God ever gave me was in providing me with a saintly mother; she was first of all a Christian mother and her chief concern was to make a good Christian out of me." (2)

His father, Pierre Berthier, called Motere, was a rugged peasant, the strict and grumbling type; he wanted his boy to receive a good education and for this purpose sent him, even as a very young child, to the Brothers of the Sacred Heart of Puys who were in charge of the village school. The school was quite a distance from the house and when little John Peter could not get there easily because of bad weather, his father used to carry him there on his shoulders.

School of the Brothers of the Sacred Heart where young Jean Berthier made his first studies; photo: Michelle Bonnard

His father, realizing that it is not enough to hand over one's son to competent teachers for an education, used to teach him at home to read and had him learn by heart many selections from the gospels. He used to experience a special delight when his little scholar succeeded in pronouncing correctly some of the most difficult names of the Holy Bible, such as Nabuchodonosor.

Fr. Berthier recalled these little incidents a few days before his death and remarked smiling: "Thus it was that I learned, even as a very little boy, to pronounce well and I can still do so today in spite of the fact that I have lost all my teeth." (3)

He was a wide-awake youngster, very precocious and had a great passion for study. As had been the case with Fr. Giraud, the pastor encouraged him and gave him his early training. The Abbé Champon chose mm as his altar boy and handed him over to his curate for his first lessons in Latin.

The youngster was gifted with an excellent memory; it was his custom on returning from Mass on a Sunday to climb on a chair and repeat word for word, and with gestures, the sermon which had been given that morning by the Curé. Fr. Champon made very good use of the little lad's oratory; every year at Mass on Palm Sunday he had the youngster recite by heart the gospel story of the Passion; this he did from his seventh to his twelfth year.

"On the other Sundays of the year", remarks the pastor's niece who had seen him perform often, "he used to ascend the steps of the communion rail when my uncle was teaching catechism after the second Mass, and little and frail as he was, he used to recite the Sunday gospel in a loud and clear voice. He was only eight years old at the time." (4)

This same contemporary of his who used to admire and observe her little friend both in the rectory and at catechism tells us how serious he used to be even then. "His modesty was most exemplary", she says. "He applied himself very diligently to his studies along with three other companions, all of whom later on became priests. He always had a book open at recreation and studied his lessons between games. He was a model for everyone at catechism, always reciting perfectly, never making a mistake." (5)

One of his little confreres was the future Bishop Gandy, Archbishop of Pondichery. Another, somewhat younger, Paul Pellet later on was Bishop of Rethymo, on the "Cotes du Benin" in Africa, and Superior General of the African Missions of Lyons. They were both great friends of Fr. Berthier. Even in those early days they dreamed of faraway mission lands and Fr. Champon encouraged them by giving them to read the Annals of the Propagation of Faith and the numerous letters he received from foreign missionaries who appealed to his generosity. (6)

To his intellectual work he added manual labor – this he will continue to do the rest of his life. He assisted his father in the cultivation of the farm during his vacations as a seminarian and he did not hesitate to work at the most tiring tasks; at four o'clock in the morning he was at work, mowing the fields or walking behind a plow. He was the oldest of six children and it was up to him to give good example.

At the Minor Seminary of Côte-Saint-André

In October 1853, after studying for some time at the rectory of Chatonnay, he went to the Minor Seminary of Côte-Saint-André, not however without stirring up complaints on the part of his father who saw in his departure the loss of a useful fellow worker. Both the pastor and his mother intervened and what a mother wants, God wants.

A burse had been established at about that time by a priest of Chatonnay and this partly removed the father's objection to the vocation of his son; thanks to this, the youngster could enter the seminary without incurring any expense on the part of the father.

Cloister at the Old Seminary in La Côte-Saint-André

He who later on was to be called the ardent apostle of vocations was made to feel the difficulties of leaving home when he himself wanted to follow his own vocation to the apostolate. (7)

He went through his early studies very quickly: he was placed in the fourth class (translator's note – the fourth class is equivalent to our sophomore year in high school) at Côte-Saint-André Seminary. He finished his courses at the Minor Seminary in 1857, and that same year went to Rondeau, to the Major Seminary where he completed his philosophical studies in one year.

He indeed moved along very fast and his biographers – without agreeing too much among them selves on what year he spent in this or that class – all agree that he completed his classical and philosophical studies at the age of 18.

He had a bit of trouble at first keeping up with the class; soon the capacity of the country boy for work and his application to studies brought him good grades with the result that in the higher classes we find him first or second in most of his subjects.

Fr. Giraud used to enjoy himself in the garden of poetry; young Berthier found his delight in the vaster and more arduous field of botany. He who later on was to be a realist and bring into actuality most important projects began by being an ardent student of the sciences, physics, minerology and geology in which he won the first prizes. One of his fellow students remarked that hiss features appeared just a little bit harsh and affected and that there was even then a professorial look about him. **(8) & (9)** "One can truly say", he adds "that Fr. Berthier has always been a teacher." One of his spiritual sons who knew him better than anyone else since he had the opportunity of studying him during his whole life corroborates this opinion, stating that "this judgment is quite exact because it is really in keeping with the temperament and character of Jean Berthier who was, we must admit, energetic and sometimes harsh, even severe, severe with himself but not with others." **(10)**

He relished philosophy much less than he did the sciences; Descartes was very popular at that time yet he could, not bring himself to rely on his philosophy. Later on, while he was at the grand seminary, he was compelled to revise his philosophical principles.

"How fortunate you are", he later on said to his spiritual sons, "to be able to study a sound philosophy, one that gives you correct ideas! I never enjoyed that happiness. In my day, nobody was spoken of but Descartes. I studied him thoroughly and I felt that there was something wrong somewhere; my mind was far from satisfied. His *Cogito, ergo sum (I think, therefore I am)* did not mean any more to me than *I eat, therefore I exist.* I never could understand what proof one could draw from that; how can thinking be a proof of our existence when it is only an effect of it? As soon as I could I began to study St. Thomas; I remade, as it were, my whole philosophy and thanks to this revision I was able to acquire a sound theology; it is here also that I became acquainted with the Fathers and the treasures which their writings contain." (11)

At the Grenoble Grand Seminary

He entered the Grand Seminary at Grenoble October 23, 1858, together with several of his friends from Chatonnay. Even forty years later he used to shed tears of joy as he recalled the emotion he felt when he crossed the threshold of that austere and tall building on Vieux Temple Street.

"I felt that I had to be alone and shed tears", he afterwards remarked to one of his intimate friends. "The thought that this very cell of mine could have been occupied by martyrs, by confessors of the faith, and certainly by saintly priests, compelled me to look upon it with

(from left) Fathers Rousselot and Orcel

respect and veneration. I could see in spirit all those who had lived there before me; it seemed to me that their virtues had made this place holy and everything about the room said to me 'be worthy of those who have lived here before you'" (12)

In order to be a worthy imitator of his predecessors he set about resolutely to follow perfectly the rules and program of the residence. All his fellow students, in the minor and major seminaries, admired him very much; one of his confreres states that "both he and Mr. Gandy (the future bishop) were models of intelligence and examples of solid virtue." (13)

Another makes the following remark about him: "he was a very hard worker, gifted with rare common sense and a modesty that was on a par with his literary and theological talents." (14)

He was also well thought of by his professors, best known of whom were Fathers Rousselot and Orcel, both outstanding teachers, the one because of the solidity of his theological doctrine, the other because of the prudence and common sense of his spirituality. As Fr. Archier had done many years before, he confided the direction of his soul to Fr. Orcel who was at one and the same time director of the seminary and Vicar General of the Diocese, a man whom Bishop de Bruillard called "a priest par excellence" and his "priest of gold." (15)

As did Fr. Archier, he kept for the rest of his life, stamped on his own soul, the marks of the vigorous spirit and the supernatural and diffusive realism of Fr. Orcel. No doubt Fr. Orcel must have recognized something of himself in his disciple when he remarked "that his piety and talents were 'very good' and that his exterior appearance was 'good enough'"; Fr. Orcel also makes the following remarks: "his health is poor but he is a serious and zealous seminarian." (16)

He worked "with great assiduity" as he himself expresses it (17) and we can easily believe that he applied himself unrelentingly to his studies. He had no preference for any particular subject, neither did he specialize in any of the ecclesiastical sciences. He wanted to know everything about theology, Sacred Scripture, Church History, etc., and his mind knew how to coordinate everything so that he might be able to better fulfill the ministry to which he would devote himself later on.

He is pictured, even in those days, as absorbed in books, extracting the matter he would later on use in his preaching and his other priestly duties. He was by nature a great one for collecting things and we see him selecting, labeling, classifying and filing with order and logic scripture texts and historical facts which he ran across during his studies.

We are told that he outlined his study plan during his seminary years always having in view what would be practical and useful in his future ministry. He took careful notes in an indexed copybook of everything in his text books, conferences, conversations, private and public reading that made an impression on him. He classified all his notes according to a definite plan; where moral matters were concerned, he noted clearly and scrupulously the shades of probability and the degrees of certitude involved." (18)

Priest and Missionary

Fr. Berthier's nephew, Antoine Berthier with his family in 1927; photo: Madame Gay.

His love of study and his piety were outstanding; because of these excellent qualities he was ordained a Deacon at the age of 21. When he was 22 he had completed all his theological studies; a dispensation was obtained from Rome and he was ordained to the priesthood by Bishop Ginoulhiac of Grenoble on September 20, 1862, in the anniversary month of Our Lady of La Salette.

His compatriots and friends were spending much time preparing for the missions, (one belonged to the Foreign Mission Society of Paris, the other to the African Missions of Lyons). Fr. Berthier on the other hand became a Missionary immediately; the Virgin of September 19, 1846, had chosen him and set him apart for herself; he was a missionary and a Missionary of La Salette even before becoming a priest.

Endnotes

(1) *Bulletin of the Missionaries of La Salette*. March 1909, p. 81; (2) From Lombaerde, *An apostle nowadays or the Life and Spirit of Fr. Jean Berthier*. Grave (1910), p. 29; (3) Ramers, *Review of the Holy Family*, in January 1928, and Garnet, Bulletin, March 1909, p. 80; (4) *Bulletin*, Ibidem, p. 82, note. From Lombaerde, cited above, p. 42. (5) Ramers, "*Review of the Holy Family*", February 1928; (6) Ramers, Ibidem, March 1928; (7) Ramers titled his study in *Review of the Holy Family: A Vocation of an Apostle and the Apostle of Vocations*; (8) De Lombaerde, cited above, p. 55; (9) De Lombaerde, cited above, p. 55; (10) Ramers, Ibidem; (11) De Lombaerde, Ibidem, p. 79; (12) Ibidem, p. 76; (13) Ibidem, p. 90; (14) De Lombaerde, cited above, p. 87; (15) De Lombaerde, cited above, p. 76; (16) Ramers, Part 1 Sources, 1st chapter, 3rd paragraph, no. 39 and also *Review of the Holy Family*; (17) De Lombaerde, cited above, p. 88; (18) Ramers, *Review of the Holy Family*.

**Jaques-Marie-Achille Ginoulhiac (1806-1875).
Bishop of Grenoble (1853-1870)**

2

First Contacts with La Salette

Fr. Berthier used to take a great delight in saying that he first heard the recital of the supernatural Apparition of La Salette from the lips of his beloved grandmother; he tells us, too, that the seeds of devotion to Mary were sown in his heart by this same grandmother, his own mother and his whole pious family.

He was not seven years old in 1846 yet he remembers well the great emotion he experienced as a child when he first heard the story of the blessed virgin speaking to the two little children. He recalls, too, how everyone was stunned by this great event.

Maximin and Melanie, the two witnesses of the La Salette Apparition

In 1861 – he was 21 at the time – he conceived the idea of getting better acquainted with the Virgin of La Salette. There was a bit of curiosity connected with this idea; there was also an ardent love for "The Beautiful Lady" who had appeared to Maximin and Melanie.

While he was at the Minor Seminary he and his friend, Gandy, were members of "the Knights of the Guard of Honor of the Virgin Mary." Every day during the month of May seven of these members used to assemble as a guard of honor and recite the rosary before a picture of their beloved Mother. (1)

It was towards the end of his grand seminary days that Fr. Berthier was to meet for the first time, on her high mountain, that Virgin who had kindled the fires of ecstasy in the hearts of the two children and he also wanted to dedicate his life to the service of this same virgin.

During the vacation which followed his ordination to the Sub-Diaconate, he set out on a pilgrimage to La Salette with six of his fellow students, among them the future bishop of Pondicherry. Towards the end of his life, he used to often recall with great delight this expedition, undertaken during his enthusiastic youth. He had prepared its every detail carefully and forty years later he could remember every incident of this exciting trip. **(2)**

"It is a long way from Grenoble to Corps", he said, "but the desire to see the place which the Blessed Virgin had watered with her tears made us oblivious of the distance and the hardships we experienced on this long walk. We finally arrived at La Salette. Once we reached the top of the mountain, all we saw there was a small statue which had been donated by a laborer of Lyons in gratitude for a miraculous cure obtained through the intercession of Mary; there were also little white wooden crosses, placed at intervals along the path which had been traced by the Blessed Virgin. There was not much there to dazzle the eyes of the body; there was very much for the eyes of the soul to see. The thought that Mary had sanctified this spot by her presence, that she had watered with her tears the very ground we were walking upon, the sight of the Missionaries who had met there to recite their breviary with the greatest devotion, all this enraptured me; on leaving I said to myself: "I will return here." **(3)**

His Call to the Holy Mountain

On his return to Grenoble he spoke to Fr. Orcel of the inward and positive call he had received from the lips of the Virgin Reconciler who befriended children, the working man and the common people. Since he was a country boy and a laborer who had worked in the fields, why should he not dedicate himself to her service?

"Let us wait and pray", answered his austere director. "Take your time and trust in God; we will speak of this matter again." **(4)**

Fr. Orcel was always suspicious of sudden spiritual enthusiasm and mistrusted any outburst of fervor that might affect the future of an individual. He pondered a long time on the new vocation of the young seminarian. He decided to speak about it to a priest in whom he had great confidence, Fr. Archier, Superior of those same Missionaries whom Abbé Berthier had admired and envied so much when he had visited the mountain.

It is interesting to note here that the vigor, the practicality and common sense of the spiritual life of both Fr. Archier and Fr. Berthier are a worthy tribute to the prudence of Fr. Orcel.

Meeting: Fr. Pierre Archier and Jean Berthier

An appointment was made and the Deacon Jean Berthier met Fr. Archier for the first time; this meeting is recorded as providential by the spiritual sons of both Fr. Archier and Fr. Berthier. **(5)**

"At first sight Fr. Archier perceived the strength of will and generosity of soul of the young deacon; "My friend" he said, "I trust that you are not afraid of crosses because the Blessed Virgin has planted quite a number of them at La Salette."

"That is exactly what I want", the young cleric replied. "If the Blessed Virgin has planted crosses, I am sure that she will send along a little sunshine to make them grow!"

Fr. Pierre Archier, M.S.
(1815-1899), first La Salette
Superior General

"Fr. Archier understood and, taking his new friend by the hand, said: "Goodbye, my friend, we will get along very well." **(6)**

"Fr. Orcel who witnessed this short but significant interview had just become the connecting link between these two great souls who would dedicate their lives to a common endeavor and achieve the greatest success therein."

"What do you think of this priest" Fr. Orcel asked Abbé Berthier. "He is indeed the man whom the Blessed Virgin needs", he answered smiling; "It must make one happy to live with a man like that; he has the innocence and modesty of a child, the energy and character of an old soldier."

"From this day there sprung up a saintly friendship between Fr. Archier and the young seminarian. These two great souls were made to love and understand each other. They had the same aspirations, the same zeal, the same spirit of self sacrifice; one could almost say that one heart beat within their breasts, that the same good angel inspired their thoughts." **(7)**

Fr. Archier was the model on which Fr. Berthier patterned his life; he was his dearest and closest friend and remained so until death; the founder of the Holy Family Community wrote as follows on June 3, 1897: "Our dear Fr. Archier is a little better today but I am fearful of the outcome because of his advanced age, 82: he is the best friend I have in the world." **(8)**

Hardly had he made his acquaintance when he chose him as his spiritual director and he completely manifested his soul to him whenever he visited the Grand Seminary. From now on he will belong to La Salette, Fr. Archier and the Blessed Virgin.

Novitiate at La Salette

The Abbé Berthier said a final goodbye to the Grenoble Seminary and his teachers in July 1862. On July 14, he went up to La Salette without visiting or even notifying his parents.

He wrote the following later on: "I decided to enter the newly founded congregation of the Missionaries of La Salette without visiting my family; I wanted to spare my parents, who would regret my not becoming a secular priest, the still greater pain of not seeing me say my first Mass in my own parish together with my two confreres, had I also been a priest." (9)

Fr. Bossan, in his *Notes on the Origin of the Community of the Missionaries of La Salette* mentions "the arrival, on Monday at 7:30, of Abbé Berthier, Deacon from Chatonnay, to become a Missionary of La Salette" and adds: "Fr. Giraud continues to be in charge of the novitiate." (10)

Later on he notes that Abbé Berthier was Fr. Giraud's second novice (11) and when his novitiate is prolonged much beyond the normal length of time because of his ill health, he refers to him as "the ex-novice of Fr. Giraud." (12)

He had been on the holy mountain but a short time when Fr. Archier handed him over to Fr. Giraud; thus it was that he went from one to the other, let us say, from action to contemplation, this period of contemplation was interrupted many times during his three years of illness or when he went out on ministry on orders from his superiors.

Fr. Giraud enjoyed the full confidence of the Superior, Fr. Archier. He devoted himself wholeheartedly to the spiritual formation of his novice who had become very much aware of the difficulties the young community was experiencing; yet he considered it a great blessing to be trained in the religious life by a master in the spirit of sacrifice.

There is no doubt that his active nature must have found it difficult to submit itself to this training, yet he applied himself with all possible good will in spite of his bad health which soon suffered a serious setback. Could we find here the reason why he was not any too enthusiastic over the ideas and the heroic methods of the austere sacrificer?

His Ordination and First Mass

In his case the beginning of the novitiate was an immediate preparation to the priesthood. On September 10, he went to Grenoble with Fr. Giraud under whose direction he had made a ten-day retreat; he was ordained, as Fr. Giraud had been, in the private chapel of the bishop together with a Carthusian Monk. **(13)**

The next morning he said his first Mass, a very quiet and private ceremony, in the temporary chapel of the Missionaries located on Neuve-des-Penitents Street. **(14)** In his humility he considered even that too good for him and he certainly reechoed the sentiments of his father master when he wrote later on; "On that day I would have liked to bury myself in a cave or go dawn to the bottom of a well to be alone, disturbed by no one, to abandon myself completely to the inspirations of the Holy Spirit." **(15)**

Fr. Berthier did not return to La Salette after his ordination; it was deemed imprudent to expose his weak constitution to the rigors of the Winter season on that mountain. He continued his novitiate in the residence of Grenoble; Fr. Henry Berthier (1833-1885), Assistant Superior, acted as Fr. Master whenever Fr. Giraud was obliged to be absent on preaching assignments. Fr. Giraud always resumed his duties as master on his return home and he continued in this capacity even after he was appointed Superior.

A Siege of Illness

After a few months, the young priest-novice was practically exhausted. He had carried on bravely during his novitiate preparing for his ordination and the religious life; he had worked beyond his strength and he could go no further. Fr. Bossan writes as follows, April 22, 1863: "Fr. Berthier has been very sick for the past two months, especially so for eight days now; he spits and vomits blood. He is very weak and pale." **(16)**

He needed immediate rest; His health, having broke down under the crosses previously predicted by Fr. Archier, had to be taken care of. What was to be done? His former spiritual directors, Fr. Orcel and Fr. Archier, were consulted and it was decided to send him home for a rest with his family at Chattonay.

This interruption of his preparation for the religious life and his return to the family which he had given up for Christ was a real sacrifice on his part. "I have dedicated myself to the Blessed Virgin", he said to those who advised him to spend some time with his family, "and I belong no longer to myself. I want to remain faithful to my vocation even though I should die." **(17)**

He agreed to leave Grenoble out of obedience, (after having had frequent hemorrhages during the previous two weeks): **(18)** on April 27, 1863, he went to Chatonnay where he received the assiduous attention of his parents, always eager however to return and take up again the exercises of his novitiate.

He returned to Grenoble the following June 2nd, "still ill and weak", **(19)** according to Fr. Bossan. He was given permission to make a pilgrimage to the holy fountain on June 16; all he did on that occasion was to pay a short visit. Immediately after this he made arrangements to go somewhere to recuperate, all the while doing some very light work.

Mental Sufferings

This illness of his was trying and painful, especially so for a young man hardly 23 years old; to make matters worse there were some rather rude remarks made to him and about him because of his physical condition. There were even some who did not hesitate to reproach him with being a burden and a hindrance to the newly-born community of Missionnaries.

This was a cause of great suffering for him: "When they sent me out of my community to recuperate", he wrote later on recalling this period of his life, "I might as well have been sent to prison or put to death." **(20)**

Tutor and Chaplain

His superiors next sent him to the Chateau de Bresson to live with the Countess de Chabons; while there he was to act as private tutor to her grandson, Eynard de Monteynard. He arrived at the Chateau on June 22, 1863, **(21)** in anything but an enthusiastic mood, "extremely embarrassed and as timid as a rat", yet not without having enjoyed one good laugh on the way; the mule on which he was riding to the castle had brushed against a thorny bush with the result that there was a one-foot rip in his cassock." **(22)**

Countess Marie-Zénaïde de Chabons

He was lonesome for La Salette and four months later, on the 20th of October, he came back to his beloved mountain and novitiate, he returned there a number of times during the nest three years, always trying to complete his novitiate.

He fell sick immediately and ten days after arriving on the mountain, the 30th of October, he was sent to another chateau where he could get some rest and still be of some service to the personnel there; he was named chaplain to the Marquise of Quinsonnaz, at the Chateau de Merieu, in Crey-Persigneux, near Morestel.

On the day of his departure our chronicler wrote as follows: "the state of Fr. Berthier's health is still very bad; he is unable to do any work." **(23)**

In the face of such evident weakness, even his best friends could do nothing for him. Providence however had its plans for the sickly novice and the time would soon come when he would accomplish great things.

He was in turn to be private tutor, chaplain, assistant in a parish and finally a full-fledged Missionary; through these different assignments he became acquainted with many phases of the priestly life and was very well prepared to attend to the spiritual needs of the Christian people confided to him by Our Lady of La Salette who first made him partake of her sufferings and then sent him forth as an apostle of her divine message.

Endnotes

(1) Ramers, Ibidem; (2) There he met two other pilgrims friends, the future rector of the Catholic Schools of Paris, Mgr d'Hulst and *Just de Bretenières* which was to be martyred in Korea on March 8, 1866. – *Life of Bishop Hulst by Bishop Baudrillart*, Paris, Poussielgue, 1912. t. 1., p. 110 and 111, and *Just de Bretenieres*, by C. Appert, Lyon, Vitte, 1910, p. 102; (3) *Bulletin*, July 1909, p. 215. De Lombaerde, cited above, p. 106; (4) De Lombaerde, cited above, p. 110; (5) Fr. Garnet, M.S.F., in the *Bulletin*, July 1909, p. 216, and De Lombaerde, M.S.F., in his *Life of Fr. Archier*, p. 117; (6) *Bulletin*, Ibidem; (7) From De Lombaerde, Ibidem; (8) Ramers, *Sources*, p. 20, no. 16; (9) De Lombaerde, cited above, p. 120; (10) Bossan, Note of July 14, 1862; (11) Bossan, Note of June 22, 1863; (12) Ibidem, Note of January 11, 1864; (13) Bossan, Note of Sept. 20, 1862, and De Lombaerde, cited above, p. 120. – Father Ramers, in support of his statement on the official register of the bishopric of Grenoble, says that Father Berthier was mistaken, because of the white habit of the two Dominicans ordained with him; (14) Then became rue St-Vincent-de-Paul, then rue Voltaire; (15) De Lombaer-

de, cited above, p. 124; (16) Bossan, Note of April 22, 1863; (17) De Lombaerde, cited above, p. 137; (18) Bossan, *Notes* of April 27, 1863; (19) Ibidem, Note of June 2nd, 1863; (20) Ramers, *Sources*, p. 23, no. 8; (21) Bossan, *Notes* of June 22, 1863; (22) Read this funny episode told by Father Berthier himself in the last days of his life: De Lombaerde, cited above, p. 142; (23) Bossan, *Notes* of October 30, 1863.

Fr. Jean Berthier M. S. (1840-1908),
Drawn on September 19th, 1890

3
At Grenoble and the Chartreuse

La Grande Chartreuse

Fr. Berthier did not remain very long at the second chateau; he returned to his community in Grenoble on January 2, 1864, after an absence of not quite three months. Chateau life weighed heavily on him; he had not been ordained a priest for that. He looked to the broader horizons of the missionary field; he wanted to cover more ground, conquer more souls.

Since he could not convince his superiors that there was a marked improvement in his health, he agreed to take some more time off – this time in a Carthusian Monastery. He had always entertained a great love for the Carthusian way of live and at one time had seriously thought of entering the Order. Was it not at the Grande Chartreuse which he had visited in 1861 that he had resolved to become a religious?

Later on he wrote as follows; "when I visited the Grande Chartreuse with a few of my fellow students, I saw there the beauty and the advantages of the religious life; from then on I had a strong desire to enter religion." (1)

He loved to recall that he had been ordained to the priesthood along side a Carthusian monk.

He remained two weeks in Grenoble; then, on January 19, 1864, he set out for the Chartreuse de Valbonne, near Pont-Saint-Esprit, in Gard. (2) The time he spent there (it extended into March) was most beneficial to him physically and spiritually.

His superiors next sent him as assistant to a sick pastor; he accepted this assignment most cheerfully, resolved more than ever to dedicate himself to the apostolate of La Salette. It was here that he prepared for the career which Divine Providence had outlined for him.

Curate at Veyssilieu

On March 30, 1864, he arrived at Veyssilieu-les-Cremieu, in the district of Tour-du-Pin, as temporary assistant to Fr. Douare.

Because of his illness the pastor no longer said Mass (3) and although it could not be helped, the parish had been neglected for quite some time. Fr. Berthier took in at a glance all the work that had to be done immediately. He admitted later on that this period of prodigious activity had been a great factor in restoring him to good health.

Church of the Castle of Veyssilieu-les-Cremieu

He himself has given us a description of his great zeal in his beautiful book, *The Priesthood*, where he outlines "the obligations of the good shepherd", the most important of which is "to know his sheep." In that book he makes mention of a certain young priest he knew very well who was attending to the spiritual needs of about 400 souls in a small parish; he indeed knew this priest very well for it was himself.

He planned his afternoon walks in such a way as to contact each family at least once a week; whenever a child missed catechism or did not come to confession with the other, if a young man failed to attend religious instruction or missed choir rehearsal, if a young girl went to the dance, he made a remark to the parents and the child concerned and it was agreed that they would do better in the future.

That parish was a typical French parish of that day; yet at the end of a year infractions of God's law were few and everyone lived up to his obligations, knowing that a check was kept on everything. When there was a special communion for the men or older boys, he called at their homes to remind them of it and, if need be, answer their objections. At the end of a year, every young man up to seventeen years of age assisted at the special religious instruction classes; the choir of the small church had eighteen good singers; on certain feast days, such as the ascension, en average of eighteen men received Holy Communion; even the youngest children went to confession regularly; no young girl dared go to the dance." (4)

That was the way he lived his twenty-fifth year, the trial period of his pastoral ministry; later on he will be able to speak and write from experience; everyone spoke very highly of the results and successes he achieved through his truly apostolic zeal. (5)

As a result of his great activity and perseverance, the complexion of the parish was completely changed; everybody assisted at Holy Mass and fulfilled all their other Christian duties. Even the most obstinate could not resist for long his captivating smile and his friendly handshake; "he is not a curé like the others, they used to say. The cabarets were practically empty and the old pastor, whose right hand he was, marveling at the changes which had taken place in such a short time, could not believe his eyes; he could not thank Our Lady enough for having sent him such invaluable help. (6)

His field of labor was extensive and included everybody; he came into contact with all classes of society, showed a great interest in their various activities, took as good care of the children as he did of the parents, organized special societies for young men, young ladies and mothers. He took on-the-spot notes of his varied activities, thus getting together material for the books he would write later on; he went indeed directly to the people as Our Lady of La Salette had urged him to do.

"Yes, my children", he later on said to the first religious of his Institute of the Holy Family as he recalled the memory of his stay in Veyssilieu: "We must go to souls, they will not come to us. We must go out and meet the people and not wait till they come looking for us." **(7)**

Elsewhere he says: "Souls do not come to God in groups; we must contact them individually; we must meet every man, every woman, every young man, young woman and child." That was the method he had outlined for himself and he followed it all his life. "Any other idea we have of the ministry", he added, "is false, or at least incomplete."

"When I was twenty-four, I gave a mission all by myself", he adds; "I was as scared as a rat at the time, yet I went out and visited all the people because I understood how necessary that was." **(8)**

Recognizing his great zeal and the wonderful success he had realized in the parish of Veyssilieu, his ecclesiastical superiors would no doubt have appointed him to parochial work; a parish however was too united an area for such an active and talented man, so Our Lady of La Salette called him to broader missionary fields, choosing him as the bearer of her message to all her people.

Return to La Salette: Profession

He returned to La Salette in June 1865, after fifteen months of tireless work which, according to one of his biographers, turned out to be a period of preparation for thirty-five years of preaching. **(9)**

The Holy Mountain of La Salette, France, in the late 1800s

"As soon as I felt that my health had been restored", he wrote later on, "I returned to La Salette. The grief I felt on leaving the good old curé was greater than that which I experienced on leaving my family; I was most anxious to return to the community which I loved and take up again my work of being a "missionary"; shortly after my return I made my religious profession and immediately took up the ministry of hearing confessions and preaching." (10)

After having, as it were, set aside the contemplation of Fr. Giraud, he now comes back to it more docile and confident than ever; he felt the need of it, both as a foundation of his future apostolate and for the better fulfillment of his ministry among souls. Fr. Giraud had been appointed Superior of the Community the preceding February 2nd while still retaining his office of Master of Novices.

Fr. Berthier wrote as follows June 22, 1865, immediately after his return to the community: "This morning Fr. Giraud went up the mountain and ordered me to remain in Grenoble for a while longer in spite of my eagerness to accompany him there; circumstances, such as they are, as well as our limited personal, required that this step be taken." **(11)**

He rejoined his Master of Novices on August 18, to complete his novitiate, one that had stretched over a period of three years, broken up frequently by painful illnesses as well as by his fifteen-month sojourn in Veyssilieu. After three months of intense preparation, he pronounced his first vows on September 8, 1865, fully dedicating himself to her who was asking him "to come near" and "make known to all her people" the message she had confided to him.

He read the following notice in the "Register of Professions" of the Community of the Missionaries of Our Lady of La Salette; "On the eighth day of September, 1865, Feast of the Nativity of the Blessed Virgin Mary, Fathers Jean Berthier and Joseph Perrin, both priests of this Diocese of Grenoble, having completed their novitiate and obtained the unanimous vote of the community, took for three years the ordinary vows of religion, conformably to the Rule of the Missionaries of Our Lady of La Salette, in the Sanctuary on the Holy Mountain, at the hands of Reverend Fr. Giraud, Superior of the Missionaries, acting in the name of the Bishop of Grenoble and delegated by him for this purpose." **(12)**

Both the bishop and his delegate acted in the name of Our Lady of La Salette who had chosen and brought together in the same ceremony, presided over by the mystical Fr. Giraud, her two most active missionaries, Fathers Jean Berthier and Joseph Perrin; these two priests were to make her September 19, 1846, message known far and wide, to the very limits of the world by means of the many missionaries whose superiors they would later on be; Fr. Perrin in his capacity of Superior General in his own institute and Fr. Berthier as the founder of a new community, known as the Missionaries of the Holy Family.

They made their religious profession at seven o'clock in the morning; on the same day one of Our Lady's future pioneers wrote in his notes "that the Superior General had received their first vows at his Mass and that he appeared quite moved." **(13)**

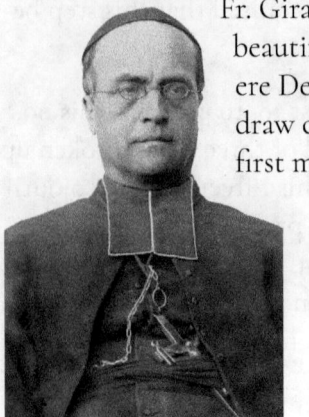

Fr. Joseph Perrin, M.S. (1836-1913), fourth La Salette Superior General

Fr. Giraud delivered the sermon and spoke of their beautiful union with God through Mary; "Adhaerere Deo mihi bonum est (It is good for me to draw close to God)"; that was Mary's life from the first moment she came into the world.

"Adhaerere Mariae mini bonum est (It is good for me to draw close to Mary)" – that should be the supreme preoccupation of a Missionary of La Salette." (14)

From now on, missionary zeal would be the driving force of Fr. Berthier's life. Illness will no longer incapacitate though it will, at times, slow down his instinctive impetuosity. Although he will suffer from painful stomach trouble the rest of his life, nothing will hinder him in the pursuit of his ideal or prevent him from working tirelessly at the many wonderful tasks he undertook for the glory of the Virgin of La Salette who had prepared him for and who now was urging him on to the apostolate of preaching and writing.

Endnotes

(1) *Bulletin*, July 1909, p. 215; (2) Bossan, *Notes* of January 11 and 19, 1864; (3) De Lombaerde, cited above, p. 147; (4) *The Priesthood*, its excellence, its obligations, its rights, its privileges, by Fr. Jean Berthier, M.S., New edition 1898, p. 729. At La Salette, at the author's home. In Lyon, Librairie Emmanuel Vitte; (5) Fr. De Lombaerde dedicates a whole chapter, which he titled, *Zeal and Sacrifice*, the tenth of the first part, at this period of his hero's life; (6) *Bulletin*, May 1910, p. 136; (7)

De Lombaerde, cited above, p. 141; (8) De Lombaerde, cited above, p. 151; (9) Ibidem, p. 151; (10) Ibidem, p. 155; (11) Letter to Fr. Douare, priest of Veyssilieu; (12) *Register of Professions*, p. 8; (13) Joseph Perrin, *Notes on the Pilgrimage*, 1st notebook, p. 72; (14) Ibidem.

4
In the Service of Our Lady and Her People

His first experience in the ministry was in a parish which he practically transformed. He had hardly become a Missionary of La Salette when he dedicated himself wholeheartedly and tirelessly to preaching and hearing confessions. He was only twenty-five years old; even then, his experience in the parochial ministry, his knowledge of its trials and difficulties was that of a priest many years his senior.

Entrance to the Chateau of Veyssilieu

For ten consecutive years, from 1865 to 1875, even during the dreadful year of 1870, there was absolutely no rest as during that period he preached missions in Grenoble and in the surrounding diocese practically without interruption.

He lost no time. He was young, his voice strong and vibrant with emotion, his spiritual direction sound, his spirit boundless and bold. The letters he wrote to his old pastor of Veyssilieu give us a very good idea of how zealously he devoted his every bit of energy to his new work. He no longer belongs to himself; he is entirely dedicated to Our Lady and her people. He writes as though on the run:

> "I am writing you a hurried word during my recreation time", this is dated November 5, 1865, and written to the Curé of Veyssilieu. "I have practically no time of my own. There are numberless confessions here. I am scheduled to preach a retreat to the Christian Brothers of Grenoble and I have no time to prepare it." **(1)**

Most of his letters are written in short, snappy phrases; he is in too much of a hurry to give them any polish. He was always eager to take up his favorite ministry and derived so much consolation from his work that he had no time to think of that precarious health of his which could take a bad turn at any time.

In the letter previously quoted he writes as follows in all humility: "I would be so happy here if only I loved God more; there is so much good to be done and I feel so little cooperative with God's grace; what a lack of interest x seem to put in my work!"

Physically I am well; in fact, I have never felt so well in all my life. I feel no pain at all in my throat and I am taking no medication at all." **(2)**

He was so completely taken up with his work that he had no time to take care of minor matters such as writing letters or sending souvenirs to friends.

In a letter dated November 12, 1865, he begins with the following abrupt introduction:

> "Please pardon this unfortunate individual who has scarcely time to breathe; **(3)** don't accuse him of being inconsiderate when he is only very busy. I am happy to be able to send you

the little souvenirs you requested; my superior has given me permission to do so. I have not yet found time to send you the engravings for the Gorier family." (4)

September 19, 1865

He had so much to attend to, matters much more pressing and important than the items just mentioned. He was still on the Holy Mountain on the 19th of September which followed his profession and he gave himself completely to the service of the pilgrims. He wrote an account of that day's activities in one of the first issues of the *Annals*.

Postcard of Feast Day celebration on the Holy Mountain of La Salette

At the end of September he wrote as follows to the Curé of Veyssilieu: "You will find in the *Annals* an account of the September 19, activities written by your humble servant. I don't know if you will recognize him in this article; however I am giving you this information beforehand; it is a bit boastful on my part to advertise myself in this way; you are the only one to whom I would dare communicate this information. I have been very busy getting that article ready and at present I have more work to do than I can handle." (5)

Reading between the lines we can readily see the role which he played in the spiritual activities of that September 19th, whether it was in the confessional which was "besieged by penitents" or at the communion rail to which the pilgrims flocked. "More than two thousand pilgrims", he wrote, "received holy communion and among them there were at least five hundred men who edified us very much by their devotion." (6)

Recalling the wonderful events of that day, he makes the following remarks at the end of the article:

> "O you who question Mary's mercy so often shown at this site and who have nothing but words of contempt and scorn in reference to her Glorious Apparition, come and take a good look at the picture I have painted for you in such an imperfect way and your minds will see the light of truth; your hearts will be touched and you will mingle your tears with those which Mary shed on this Mountain and you will proclaim with us this prodigy of Mary's clemency." (7)

Letter to the Curé of Veyssilieu

The wonderful things which happened at the Holy Mountain were a solid proof of the Apparition of La Salette. He was however always dreaming greater dreams and could not understand the evasive attitude of an old-fashioned and too considerate prudence. In that same letter where he gives a rapid fire account of his multiple and unceasing activities, he makes a strong attempt at rousing his old pastor out of his lethargy and advises him to be more zealous and active.

The poor old pastor was always sick; at least he thought he was. Here are some of the prodding phrases Fr. Berthier wrote him: "A little courage and effort and you will find yourself above water! At least do something to help yourself! How can you allow your men's meeting to he dropped? I am unable to figure you out; I hear that you never say a word in church for fear of offending somebody. If I were only a few hours away, how I would like to hold a sword to your ribs and prod you on to a bit of action!" **(8)**

In December he wrote as follows; "How can you be so concerned about your own troubles when there is so much to be done? 'Lift up your eyes and see that the fields are ripe and ready for the harvest . . . There is an abundant harvest'. Come now, be a good laborer in the vineyard. **(9)** *Confortare et esto robustus* (*Be strong and courageous*)." **(10)**

He even went so far as to point out the hymns he should have his congregation sing. "Prepare a jubilee for the parish and preach it as you are well able to do; preach on the great truths. *Clama, ne cesses* (*Cry aloud, do not cease*)." You could close it on Christmas Day; that is what I intend to do at Saint-Prim where, according to present plans, I will be preaching. Have your congregation sing at full voice; *Avant de quitter notre mere* (*Before leaving our Mother*),

"It is a wonderful thing to be young!", wrote the old Curé. "It is indeed", answered Fr. Berthier, using the Curé's same exclamation, "but one thing about youth, and I reproach myself on this score, is that it is blessed with more activity than virtue. Yet it is so true that one must labor as a good soldier of Christ and fight the good fight of the faith. **(11)** In spite of what may be said to the contrary, it is never difficult to do good; with a little more courage along with skillful prudence ,you could do much, at least in a negative manner to prevent much evil and you could possibly bring about a real positive betterment of present conditions." **(12)**

He was always wary of his intrepid youth; he whipped it and lashed it with continual reproaches in order to keep it under control lest it lead him astray. In all humility he made every effort possible to direct it towards that that objective which his apostolic vocation had set before him. He kept his ardent enthusiasm, always eager for quick success and results, under good control and inspired by his Beautiful Lady of September 19, he made use of his enthusiastic and enterprising spirit to make her message known,

His First Book

Young Fr. Berthier's impetuous enthusiasm manifested itself at the time he published his first book. He had not dilly-dallied at all in the composition of his work and he expected that there would be no dilly-dallying on the part of others in printing it and in offering it to the public. What writer – be he humble or ambitious – isn't anxious to be recognized and does not complain when he runs into delays!

Fr. Berthier was not in such a great hurry through ambition; in his

NOTRE-DAME
DE LA SALETTE
SON APPARITION, SON CULTE
LE
PÈLERINAGE NATIONAL
DE 1872
PAR LE PÈRE J. BERTHIER
Missionnaire de N. D. de la Salette.
AVEC L'APPROBATION DE MGR L'ÉVÊQUE DE GRENOBLE

> Eh bien, mes enfants, vous le ferez passer à tout mon peuple.
> (Paroles de N.-D. de la Salette.)

PARIS
VICTOR PALMÉ, LIBRAIRE-ÉDITEUR
RUE DE GRENELLE-SAINT-GERMAIN, 25
1872

Fr. Berthier's 160-page book of 1872, *Novena in Honor of Our Lady of La Salette*, which includes historical notes

case there was no question of making a literary debut in a hostile and critical world; behind his efforts to have the book published were primarily the good of souls and the glory of God.

He wrote as follows to his former pastor at Veyssilieu, urging him to do all he could to have the book published; "Let us do our best and do that out of love of God. I hope that this little book will be read, blessed by God and do much good. This should be a good reason for us to hasten its publication since there is nothing else standing in the way." (13)

Fr. Giraud must be given credit for starting him off on his literary career. The great mystic had recognized in his novice a man of action, one who could later on do the Lord's work through both the spoken and the written word. He would be an apostle and an evangelist.

Fr. Giraud had just published a pamphlet on mental prayer; he took this, presented it to Fr. Berthier and said: "take this pamphlet and develop the thoughts contained therein; there is enough matter in it for a whole book." The novice got busy and his efforts were crowned with success. (14)

Meanwhile the novice fell sick; but that made no difference. Fr. Giraud suggested that he take up a hobby, one that would be useful and enjoyable, namely, collecting material for possible future books. This would help to while away many of his leisure hours and also expend some of that surplus energy of his.

Later on he wrote, recalling these particular novitiate days; "One of my superiors, seeing that I was too weak to do any active ministry and realizing that I had plenty of time for study, advised me to do some writing. This I did in spite of the fact that I preferred the more active works of the ministry. It is thanks to my illness – and, we may add, thanks to his superior, Fr. Giraud – that my books have done any good for, had I been well, I never would have thought of writing." (15)

It was in the first chateau where he had gone to recuperate that he conceived the topic of his first book. He was not quite twenty-four years old and it took a good deal of bold initiative on the part of the young priest to write a book treating of "The Duties of the Christian Mother towards her children, her husband and her servants."

He was helped very much in this work by the wonderful example of the devout Christian woman with whom he was living and whom he was assisting in the education of her large family. The countess Zenaide de Chabon had chosen him as tutor of her grandson, Eynard de Monteynard; while he lived there, he had continually before him the example of the countess whom forty years later he described as a very intelligent woman I knew well, mother and grandmother of noble and religious children", (16) "a true mother according to the mind of God, one who lived in the world, yet knew how to rise above the spirit of the world through her great faith." (17)

While admiring her as the type of the strong woman and perfect head of the household, he outlined a description of this woman, unknown to her, and submitted it to her for approval; he had collaborated with her and now she was to be his helper.

He wrote as follows on July 29, 1865, to the Curé of Veyssilieu; "I have handed over my manuscript to Madame de Chambons; she and her daughter, Madam de Monteynard, read it over and over again, scrupulously marking every word that had to be changed, etc., etc... Both of them urged me to publish my work and I rely on their judgment in this matter much more than I do on the opinion of many others. Indeed I believe that they are able to appreciate a work of this type better than many ecclesiastics because of the knowledge they have of people with whom they associate." (18)

He was quite conscious of the importance of this work, all the more so because of the approval of the Countess. He began the book while at the home of the Countess and finished it at Veyssilieu, writing during his spare time; he looked upon this work as a rest and distraction from his many parochial activities. Later on in a letter to his former cure, he stated with a slight tinge of malice as he tried to prod him into doing some work; "At Veysselieu there is plenty of time to write books, for it is there that I wrote my first work." **(19)**

When he returned to his community in June 1865, to complete his novitiate, the book was finished and he immediately took steps to have it printed. He had Fr. Giraud, his superior, read the manuscript and then submitted it to the chancery.

House of Berthier and his family in Chantonnay, France

"It seems that the good God wants me to publish my book soon", he wrote to the curé of Veyssilieu on July 22, "as everything required to have the book published at an early date is moving along so smoothly." In spite of this bright outlook, he will have to wait almost a year.

He wrote as follows on July 29: "Fr. Mussel told me that he had given the bishop a good report on my work, both as regards the matter and its division, since than, I have made quite a few corrections. I am to see the bishop tomorrow and I am confident of his approbation." **(20)**

In the same letter he asks Fr. Douare to handle the arrangements for the printing of his book and to find a publisher who would give him the best price. He acquainted him with whatever resources he had on hand and suggested that the best way to advertise the book would be to place it in the hands of several booksellers since each one would be interested in giving it a good write-up. He dreaded a possible lack of sale for his book and he did not want it to suffer the same fate as did Fr. Giraud's, *Vie d'Union*; here is what he wrote on this point: "Here, in Grenoble, books seem to remain in their shipping cases; we sell about three copies of the *Vie d'Union* every two weeks." **(21)**

"The community seems willing enough to take care of the printing; to be honest, I would much prefer that you handle this deal yourself since you are familiar with this sort of business – also because of my parents, please let me know by return mail if you are willing to take charge of this affair. I will then speak to Fr. Giraud and let him know that he either can take care of the printing himself or give me permission to have you do so." **(22)**

His former pastor of Veyssilieu gladly consented to handle this matter for him; our young author however was always in a hurry and during the final months of his novitiate the publication of his book seemed to preoccupy him constantly; he kept running back and forth to the chancery to obtain the required approbation and sent letter after letter to Fr. Douare for help.

On August 10, he wrote the latter as follows: "I have made so many trips to the bishop's house, because of my book, that I dare not show my face there again." **(23)** He doesn't forget a thing; in that same letter he mentions the size and shape of the book, insists that it must be a neat printing job. "As soon as we have our books, it would be a good idea to send some copies to convent schools for the opening of the scholastic year in October so that the mothers who accompany their children there might obtain a copy. We could also interest convent Superiors and directresses of boarding schools by sending them complimentary copies. These should not be too expensive, about 1 franc 10 or 1 franc 15 for the book printed on cheaper paper and 1 franc 25 or 1 franc 27 for that printed on the better grade. Our chief aim must be to do as much good as possible…" **(24)**

The book was still a long say from this projected advertising campaign, even a long way from being printed. The author was becoming more and more impatient and was leaving the blame for the delay on his old pastor to whom he had sent the manuscript.

He wrote again at the end of September, inquiring how things were coming along and what offers had been made to him. "Try and hurry this business along and bring it to an end", he said rather roughly; "I am giving you full power of attorney; should you be unable to make suitable arrangements, I will have the printing done in Grenoble. It is not a matter of making any money; whether I make anything or not, God be praised!" **(25)**

Font in which Fr. Berthier was baptized

No progress at all was being made and Fr. Berthier was on pins and needles because of the delay. Finally a publisher in Lyons was contacted, a Mr. Josserand, and Fr. Giraud handed over the manuscript to him. Mr. Josserand seemed to be as tantalizingly inactive as had been the Abbé Douare and the young priest blasted them both with his most vehement reproofs and scoldings.

"I hardly know what to say about Mr. Josserand", he wrote to his former pastor of Veyssilieu on November 5, 1865, "for mercy's sake, please stir up things so that at least some little bit be accomplished; we have lost so much time already. I wrote to him recently, about three weeks ago, entreating him to hurry and asking him to make all arrangements with you as I had given you power of attorney; he did not even answer me. Has your friend Mr. Boellu returned yet? Please write to him and let us finish this business once and for all; it has been dragging on much too long." **(26)**

It was still to drag on through the whole Winter. Satisfactory terms were finally agreed upon; even then there seemed to be no end to the time the actual printing took. Fr. Berthier practically stomped with rage and complained to his friend at Veyssilieu that this affair was dragging on much beyond reason. "Everyone here", said he, "who is acquainted with our problem is convinced that these preliminaries are taking intolerably long and I am sure that you are of the same opinion. As for me, I am presently busy with other matters (he did not lose sight of the printing of his book however) and while bemoaning the fact that six months have been lost (he had finished the book six months before) I am unable to devote any time to this matter of having my book printed, as much as I would like to. Please try again and see what you can do. By the looks of things, it will take longer to get the book printed than it took to write it. Did we hand over these pages to the publisher to have them hidden away in his desk forever?" **(27)**

He was obviously losing patience and Fr. Ramers does not hesitate to show a little lack of reverence in regards to his founder by pointing out that "his choleric temperament evidently betrayed itself at this time" because others were too slow about seeing to the publication of his book. **(28)**

At last in December 1865, the printing of the book began; it progressed very slowly until March of the following year. Fr. Perrin, a confrere novice of his, informs us that in March 1866, "Fr. Jean Berthier's beautiful book, *La Mère Selon le Coeur de Dieu (The Mother according to the Heart of God)*, in-18, 500 pages, was presented to the public." **(29)** Fr. Perrin does not seem any too excited over this event and very nonchalantly announced the appearance of the book in the same paragraph in which he notes "the arrival on the mountain of Frederic, the Italian carpenter." **(30)**

The publication of his book relieved him of much worry and also of much friendly teasing on the part of his confreres. This was his hour of triumph and it was now his great hope that the book would meet with the distribution he dreamed it would have. He worked his hardest to advertise the book and promote its sale; he still kept on reproaching his old friend, the Curé, for his lack of interest in his regard. "You don't seem to be interested in me or in anything that I do", he wrote him in December 1866. "Good Lord, we can no longer rely on people nowadays." **(31)**

He had relied very much on the help of Our Lady of La Salette; had he not tasted the dregs of disappointment while on the mountain at the feet of his Weeping Mother? He had dedicated his literary apostolate to her and he was confident that she would have it bear fruit.

"My dear pious mothers", he wrote in the introduction of his book. "I have written this book in order to dry a few of Mary's tears and to help you to understand her mercy... **(32)** Kindly overlook the imperfections you will find in this work, remembering that the author wrote it to cooperate, with the Blessed Virgin in her mission here below which is to bring about your salvation and that of your children." **(33)**

There were, of course, critics; some saw no connection at all between La Salette and the matter treated in his book.

Mr. Postel wrote as follows in the *Bibliographie Catholique* of July 4, 1866; "Christian mothers will make Fr. Berthier's work their handbook; they will find therein not only exhortations, information, and advice, but also a collection of prayers and devotional exercises adapted to their needs. What reason did the author have in linking his book to the Apparition of Our Lady on the mountain of La Salette? We see no particular connection between the two." **(34)**

A Golden Chain

This criticism was superficial and uncalled for; had these critics been able to look into the future, they would have seen how well this link was connected with the others to follow, forming as it were a golden chain, a synthesis of incomparable doctrine, all contained in the teaching of La Salette.

Anticipating this criticism, he answered it beforehand and later on vindicated himself by the publication of new books.

He wrote to his fellow worker of Veyssilieu on November 12, 1865: "I will introduce more of La Salette in my future works than I did in my first book." **(35)**

He was now more than ever imbued with the spirit of La Salette because he felt that he was a better servant of his Lady who had captivated his heart. This he demonstrated in his daily life and in his books. From now on, book will follow upon book just as missions and retreats succeeded each other without interruption; henceforth Fr. Berthier's life will be one of missionary apostolate through both the written and spoken word.

Endnotes

(1) Collection of letters from Fr. Jean Berthier (1865-66) to Father Douare, parish priest of Veyssilieu-les-Crémieu (Isère), a copy of which was graciously given to the author by Father Ramers, 6th letter; (2) Ibidem, 6th letter; (3) In the sense of *hard, rigid*, as they say to *make a fresh warning*; (4) Ibidem, 7th Letter; (5) Ibidem, 4th Letter; (6) *Annals*, Sept. 1865, p. 74; (7) *Annals*, Ibidem, p. 76; (8) Ibidem, 4th letter; (9) John 4: 35, 38a; (10) Deuteronomy 31:6; (11) 2 Timothy 2:3; (12) Ibidem, 10th letter; (13) 3rd letter of August 10th, 1865; (14) De Lombaerde, cited above, p. 144; (15) De Lombaerde, cited above, p. 143; (16) *Happy pure hearts*, by Fr. Berthier, M.S,. Paris, House of Good Press (1902), p. 127; (17) *The mother according to the heart of God*, by Father Berthier, MS, Paris, House of the Good Press, 5th edition, (1898), p. 235; (18) Letters to the Fr. Douare, 2nd letter, Saturday, July 19th, 1865; (19) 7th letter, Nov. 12, 1865; (20) 2nd letter; (21) Ibidem; (22) 2nd letter; (23) 3rd letter; (24) Ibidem; (25) 4th letter; (26) 6th

letter; (27) 8th letter; (28) Letters to Fr. Douare, Explanatory Notes by Fr. Ramers, M.S.F., no. 6, p. 3; (29) Perrin, *Notes on the Pilgrimage*, first notebook, p. 109; (30) Ibidem; (31) 15th Letter to Fr. Douare; (32) Introduction of the 1st edition, p. xi; (33) p. xvi; (34) Extract from the *Catholic Bibliography*, July 1866; (35) 7th letter.

Pilgrims make their way up to La Salette in the 1870s

Foundation of a School for Missionaries

The first missionaries were not long in realizing that the laborers in the Master's vineyard were always the same few and that their number was not increasing according to their work. Fr. Berthier mentions this later on and he knew well of what he wrote, having been an eyewitness to the above mentioned state of affairs. "Crowds flock to La Salette from everywhere by the thousands", says he, "sinners are being converted and there is a definite, visible spiritual revival. All this was a source of great comfort to the Missionaries in their difficult labors . . . For twenty-five years now, from 1852 until the present time, these same Missionaries, living under the patronage of the bishops of Grenoble, have been preaching missions and retreats in this diocese and the neighboring ones and they have been blessed in their work by her who has sent them. The number of Missionaries however is far from sufficient to meet the demands of the pastors who ask for their services; to make matters worse, vocations to the priesthood are becoming fewer and fewer. **(1)**

Pilgrims gather on the Holy Mountain on Sept. 19, 1890 around the statues of the three phases of the Apparition

The recently founded Institute of the Missionaries, made up of priests and deacons from the diocese and elsewhere had no organized recruiting system; members joined it easily and left just as easily. Fr. Archier was the only one who had been there from the early days of 1852, or practically the only one. He was doing his best to hold together and train men of good will like Fr. Giraud and the other younger priests such as Fr. Jean Berthier and Fr. Joseph Perrin.

Something had to be done to secure help for these evangelical workers; but where find the necessary recruits? There was talk of founding and organizing a missionary school and this idea must have been in the minds of all since everyone was of the opinion that something had to be done to remedy this lack of missionaries.

"The Missionaries decided to found a school for boys who, though poor in the things of this world, were rich in the blessing of a priestly vocation." (2)

We can honestly say that the Superior, Fr. Archier, felt more than anyone else the urgent need and necessity of a more effective recruiting system because he personally had suffered acutely from the lack of personnel.

Fr. Archier was in full accord with their plan of founding an Apostolic School; he was opposed in this by Fr. Giraud who had other ideas about the reorganization of the Institute.

Fr. Giraud was relieved of his Superiorship on February 10, 1876, and Fr. Archier became Superior for the second time; one of his counselors was Fr. Jean Berthier who, now more than ever, was looking forward to a fuller and more successful apostolate. He, more than anyone else, was the driving force behind Fr. Archier as well as his greatest helper in the Apostolic School project which necessarily had to be put into execution if they wanted to comply with the concluding words of Mary's conversation with the shepherds of La Salette: *Well, my children, you will make this known to all my people.*

Commenting on these words of Our Lady, Fr. Berthier makes the following statement: "These words are both a resume and a conclusion of her message, and to me they express the chief purpose of her apparition at La Salette; namely, that Mary wanted to establish an apostolic center on her mountain from which vocations to the Missionary life would go everywhere to make her message known." (3)

It might be a difficult and touchy matter to explain this decision of the community to the Bishop; in this proposed school for future priests, there could be duplication of work and possibly competition with his own seminary.

Bishop Fava had just been appointed to the See of Grenoble; he was a missionary bishop par excellence who would understand very well the impatient and justifiable zeal of other Missionaries. He immediately showed a great interest in the small community of La Salette, permitting it "to establish itself on a solid basis and to organize itself as 'a real religious congregation, governing itself under a Rule'." (4)

They availed themselves of the Bishop's friendliness to ass for authorization to open up a small school at the Holy Mountain. Fr. Archier brought to these interviews the skillful diplomacy of his simplicity and good nature; Fr. Berthier too was there to lend support to his Superior and to assist him in answering the many objections of some of the members of the bishop's administration who did not look with a favorable eye on this latest step of the young community.

Bishop Fava, who had a truly apostolic heart, graciously approved the enterprise. (5) Another truly apostolic man, Fr. Berthier was given the work of putting this project into execution.

Master Recruiter and Organizer

He had had practically ten years of uninterrupted experience in preaching missions; this should be a great help to him in assisting others to become imitators of his zeal. In his book, *Etats de Vie Chretienne (Various States of the Christian Life)*, which appeared in 1874, he sets forth excellent considerations on the choice of a state of life and discusses the most important subject of vocation to the priesthood. He had the background necessary to be a master recruiter and a capable trainer of young boys preparing for the priesthood.

Fr. Archier meets with workers on the Holy Mountain

Besides this he enjoyed the full confidence of his Superior whose intimate friend and official counselor he was. Fr. Archier, a practical man, did not hesitate one moment. He saw that Fr. Berthier was the ideal man for this position and gave him charge of this project with orders to start working on it immediately.

It was a great sacrifice for him to interrupt his active missionary life to take up this humble and hidden task. He put every ounce of his tireless energy into it and worked with such zeal that the success of this enterprise was practically assured. **(6)**

At times this work will take up every spare moment he has; in fact, he made this work so much his own as to incline others to believe that he was the only one concerned with it; this was not the case however and we see him giving due credit to all the Missionaries when he wrote that "without interrupting their work at the Sanctuary, they gave practically all their free time to these dear youngsters, *the hope of the flock.*" **(7)**

We must admit however that he was the hardest worker as well as the most competent one in this undertaking. He worked passionately at this community effort; being a genius at organization, he was able to bring this project to a successful issue in spite of practically insurmountable obstacles.

He immediately went to Avignon to make an on-the-spot study of the first Jesuit Apostolic School which Fr. Alberic de Foresta, S.J. (1818-1876) had just established there. His keen mind carefully scrutinized every detail connected with a school of this type. He set about his task with his customary enthusiasm; there was much to be done, such as providing teaching personnel, recruiting students and finding the financial assistance necessary to carry on this enterprise – and there was not such time.

Pamphlets announcing this new project were mailed everywhere; he appealed to the working class for vocations from among their children and called upon the generosity of the middle class for funds to help educate these boys for the priesthood. The *Annals* of La Salette officially announced in the July issue, 1876, "that the Missionaries of La Salette were opening a special school for young men who felt attracted to the apostolic priesthood; this was being done in order to recruit members for their own community and to do what they could to keep many precious vocations from being lost. The school was to open the following August under the direction of the Fathers themselves. **(8)**

They had to work very fast. The impetuous temperament of Fr. Berthier betrays itself in the above article announcing the opening of the new school – he no doubt wrote most of it himself. This announcement had been approved by Fr. Orcel as the Bishop was absent at the time. One is led to believe that both Fr. Archier and Fr. Berthier must have made a good impression at the chancery since they allowed this project to move along so fast.

The Fathers intended to have their students advance as quickly as possible in their studies and wanted them to receive uninterrupted training in the Christian virtues; **(9)** several strict disciplinary regulations were announced beforehand, as for example that they were not to return to their families for Summer vacation; the reason for this was to gain time in their studies and eliminate many dangers they would be exposed to.

St. Joseph School near Corps

In the August issue of the annals Fr. Berthier published much useful information and answered many possible objections in his *Answers to questions relative to the School of the Missionaries of Our Lady of La Salette.* (10)

He wrote as follows: "When the humble Congregation of the Missionaries of Our Lady of La Salette accepts children in the hope of keeping them forever, it is only living up to the tradition handed down to us from the centuries of faith; it is also following the instructions of great Catholic teachers and is imitating what is done, and with good results, in a large number of recently founded congregations. – We believe that in following this procedure, we are going along according to the designs of Our Lady of La Salette who made use of two children to make known her teachings and her tears to all her people." (11)

Success of the Apostolic School

The number of applications for admission was far greater than they had hoped for. "Already", writes Fr. Berthier in this same article of the *Annals*, "we have had to put on the waiting list a number of children who desire earnestly to consecrate themselves to Our Lady of La Salette, waiting for the day when charitable souls will come to their assistance. **(12)** He relied much on the charity of "souls devoted to Our Lady of La Salette" who by increasing their offerings would thereby increase the number of students.

August 5, 1876, was announced as the opening day. A short time after that, Fr. Berthier wrote as follows: "Happy Day! Exactly one month after we announced the opening day of our school, the first fifteen students arrived at the mountain on August, Feast of Our Lady of the Snows." **(13)**

Fr. Berthier remarked that the spirit of God seemed to attract these dear young souls to Mary's Mountain and that Mary herself, who thirty years before had called the two young shepherds, was now speaking to other children, almost as poor as the first two, calling them to be messengers of her mercifulness.

"God's blessing on our work was clearly manifested", adds Fr. Berthier, not only by the conduct of our young 'postulants' but also by the large number of applications which were coming to us from everywhere. We were forced to limit the number of admissions, accepting only twenty the first year." **(14)**

The success of this apostolic work, begun on the Holy Mountain on August 5, 1876, was due to the hard work and solicitude of its chief organizer, Fr. Berthier. He was to work very hard for many years to come in order to support it, keep it going and ultimately bear fruit.

Much work had been done; everything, such as classrooms, student quarters, teachers, had to be improvised and that on a mountain thronged with numerous pilgrims whose many needs required the attention of all the Missionaries. Fortunately it was vacation time and after a short retreat the first students settled in their quarters as best they could; they were of great help in providing the singing and serving at the various ceremonies taking place at the Basilica.

"From the very beginning", states he who had been entrusted with their spiritual formation, "they cultivated habits of silence, modesty and recollection, especially in the holy places, all of which greatly edified the pilgrims. On August 15 they received the cassock, a much sought after reward for their application to work and their good behavior." **(15)**

Apostolic School at St. Joseph

Young students of Saint Joseph School

They remained on the Holy Mountain far into the Winter; it was after the Christmas holidays that they came down to Saint-Joseph, near Corps, where a more comfortable home had been prepared for them. This is where the Apostolic School was established and it was to be there for many years. Fr. Berthier accompanied his youngsters to the new school (he used to call the students his fledglings) and for five years he worked his hardest to feed this first brood" **(16)** as an eyewitness testifies.

He became local Superior of the residence on February 2, 1879, the very day he took his perpetual vows in the Institute; it is here that during five years he made use of his unusual skill and ability as a director and inspirer to make his school one that was a model of work and piety, one he was justly proud of and which he continually improved and beautified through the generosity of his benefactors.

He wrote for their benefit a little book wherein we can follow the vicissitudes of the school in its early days, admire the foresight and organization of Fr. Berthier as well as his devotion to his students. (17)

"He was their director", writes an eyewitness, "yet he was more of a father to them. He was always in their midst, teaching them, encouraging and urging them on by his kind words and good example; he was with them at chapel, study and recreation, always giving them an example of regularity and zeal." (18)

The school was given the name of "Saint Joseph"; it was also placed under the protection of this saint. Fr. Berthier had decided that the breadwinner of the Holy Family would also be the provider of his little family which was in a special way consecrated to the Blessed Virgin. Many times and in marvelous ways did he come to their assistance after they had made a novena in his honor." (19)

He did not leave everything to the good Saint however; on the contrary he wanted to be worthy of his assistance and that is why he worked very hard all the time. "When I was in charge of the Apostolic School", he confided towards the end of his life to a friend of his, "we were indeed very poor and as our boys were not recruited from the families of the wealthy, we had to tax our ingenuity to keep alive. I never begged from anybody; when charitable persons interested themselves in us, I gladly accepted their offerings. I never asked for anything. Thanks be to God, we always had what was absolutely necessary and Divine Providence never suffered us to be wanting in anything. We did everything possible, of course, to help ourselves; roasted quail does not come to anyone, cooked and ready to eat. One must take the trouble to go out and hunt them." **(20)**

He did his utmost to take care of the needs of the school, working very hard in the garden or in the fields along with the students during their recreations and congés (that is, holiday outings). He conceived all sorts of devices, such as albums and flower collections which were sold as souvenirs at the Pilgrimage and thus provided some revenue for the school. These along with the proceeds from the sale of his books helped to feed the entire community and pay for current expenses.

Very often when he was not handling a rake or a spade, he would take his alpenstock (walking-stick) and go for a climb up the mountain. He was always a collector at heart and his love for the natural sciences would come alive again whenever he walked through the woods or along the flowery mountainside.

"Recalling these trips, he later on related that in the Spring, as the snows of the mountain began to melt, he would take a few boys with him and by way of recreation gather herbs and flowers; these were afterwards pasted on printed cards and sold as souvenirs at the Pilgrimage. "This was something that took very little time", he said, "and many would consider it insignificant because of the small value of these cards, yet by means of this stratagem, I was able to pay for the board of two or three apostolics." **(21)**

Growth of the School

In this way and through other devices – (he went out quite often to preach missions and on these journeys he picked up some financial aid or signed up some new recruit) – the apostolic family was able to increase its number and strength.

"At the end of 1877", he notes in his little propaganda book which gave out information on the school, "w had over 30 boys; a few young men who had finished their classical course joined our ranks for philosophy and theology. Our apostolic project was well on its way and

Bps. Van den Branden (upper center) and Bernard Bernard, M.S. (upper left) for Ordination of La Salettes on Aug. 2, 1888 in Cathedral in Trondheim, Norway, the first since the Reformation

even now had its various branches." **(22)**

It developed very rapidly. "In January 1884, our enterprise counted more than 110 young men located in France, Norway and Switzerland. One had been ordained to the priesthood, forty or more were studying philosophy or theology; among them there were three deacons and 11 subdeacons." **(23)**

"In January 1887, Fr. Berthier's apostolic family had one hundred and fifty young men. Nineteen had been ordained priests; five of these were laboring in the Mission of Norway, more than forty were in philosophy and theology, among them many deacons and sub-deacons." **(24)**

"In a few years", writes the confident director, "we expect to average about ten ordinations to the priesthood a year if we continue to receive charitable assistance; this number will double later on if the generosity of our benefactors also doubles. Among the students who have left us, three are at the Major Seminary, one at the Missions d'Afrique, many with the Brothers of the Christian Schools, a good number in various Minor Seminaries and many others, let us hope, are in heaven." **(25)**

That is a good summary of what was accomplished in the early years of the school as well as a proof of excellent results. Bishop Fava visited the school as early as 1877, giving his blessing and encouragement to the students. Among other things, he told them that he was anxiously awaiting the day when he would ordain them to the priesthood." (26)

The Bishop made frequent visits to the seminary "and the boys loved him as a father" writes Fr. Berthier. "We feel sure that the venerable pontiff derived much consolation from his visits; we have seen him shed tears of joy as the seminarians sang special songs to welcome and honor him." (27)

Another visit excited quite a bit of enthusiasm in the little cenacle; it was that of a missionary from faraway who had come to appeal to their young and eager apostolic spirit.

"When Bishop Bernard, Prefect Apostolic of Norway and Lapland, visited our school for the first time", relates Fr. Berthier, "the students were told that the bishop was in great need of missionaries and all those who would be willing to leave with aim for that mission were asked to give in their names. All handed in their names in writing except two, and these left the seminary shortly after; no doubt they lacked the generosity required to carry on the work of the Blessed Virgin. The rest of the students had even now a truly apostolic spirit." And he wrote from personal knowledge. "Some were even moved to tears on learning that the Norwegians have no love of the Blessed Virgin and do not pray to her." (28)

Later, on the occasion of the departure ceremonies for the first missionaries leaving for Norway and Lapland which took place on the Holy Mountain on June 18 and 19, 1880, all these children of the Weeping Virgin's family were much impressed and deeply moved." (29)

This distant mission which had been confided to the care of Bishop Bernard was in great need of missionary workers and the Bishop Prefect had so much faith in the future of the Missionaries of La Salette that he asked and obtained permission from Rome to have them as collaborators in this field." (30)

A Legion of Apostles and Their Leader

"From that day on", writes the Director, "the Norway mission held a most powerful attraction for all of us who aspired to become other Francis Regises and Xaviers – this applies to the Director more so than to anyone else. As childish as was my own personal ambition, this great desire of mine to go to the missions was but a little flame compared to the impatient eagerness that had captivated our Apostolics. Vainly did we throw objections at them such as the rigors of the polar climate, the deserts of snow and ice, the hardships of isolation in a strange land, the antipathy of heretics, etc., etc.; all these objections were easily taken care of by their naive and sometimes surprising answers. We had been under the impression up to that time that all we had in the school was students whose future was more or less uncertain; we now discovered that we had a legion of apostles, clearly showing signs of a divine call." (31)

Fr. Jean Berthier, M.S.

Fr. Berthier was practically a legion in himself. His first biographer describes him "at this period of his life, that is from his ordination to his departure for Switzerland, as a man of extraordinary activity. At one and the same time he was Assistant General, local Superior, a missionary who was as often in parishes as he was on the Holy Mountain and the author of many books; he seemed to be practically everywhere. He multiplied himself tenfold and did much work at night so as to leave nothing unfinished. In spite of his multiplicity of enterprises, he accomplished each of them with unusual perfection and polish." (32)

He directed his every effort to the training of his young legionaries of Our Lady who not too long after their organization would be heard from in the most distant battle fields of the apostolate and would make known in Switzerland, in Norway and Lapland the message of their heavenly Mother who had appeared in tears on September 19, 1846. (33)

A few years later, after checking up on what had happened to the youngsters who had been so thrilled by the departure ceremonies of June 18, 1880, Fr. Berthier, their leader, remarked that up to now everyone of these dear youngsters had persevered; of the seven most advanced students one had been ordained on June 29, 1882, and was presently a Missionary in Lapland; the other six who now spoke Norwegian were finishing their studies for the priesthood in the residence of Trondheim, former capital of Norway, where they had been placed by the Bishop." (34)

"We can truly repeat with Fr. Berthier that this project seems to be in keeping with the merciful plan of the Virgin of La Salette who wanted children to make known her teachings to *all her people*." (35)

We can well add that the Blessed Virgin had Fr. Berthier in mind as the man to promote this special enterprise of hers; namely, the recruiting of children, training them and thus raising am army of numberless apostles who would establish everywhere "the peace of Christ." (36)

Endnotes

(1) *Annals of Our Lady of La Salette,* March 1877; Article reproduced in *The Work of Vocations at La Salette* by Fr. J. Berthier, Missionary of

La Salette. New augmented edition. Baratier and Dardelet, Grenoble (1884), page 6; (2) Ibidem, p. 7; (3) *The Work of Vocations at La Salette*, p. 3; (4) *Register of professions*. Session of Jan. 29, 1876, p. 21; (5) *The Work of Vocations at La Salette*, p. 7; (6) *The Work of Vocations at La Salette*, p. 50; (7) Ibidem; (8) *Annals*, July 1876, p. 606 and 607; (9) Ibidem, p. 607; (10) Ibidem, August 1876, p. 609 and following. Article borrowed by Fr. Berthier for his own book on *States of Christian Life*, chapter 13, p. 186, 1st edition; (11) Ibidem, p. 611; (12) Ibidem, p. 613; (13) *The Work of Vocations at La Salette*, p. 18; (14) Ibidem, p. 18; (15) Cited above, P. 19; (16) De Lombaerde , cited above, p. 189; (17) All of this beautiful book is to be read, edited several times and each time with new interesting details; (18) De Lombaerde, cited above, p. 190; (19) *The Work of Vocations at La Salette*, p. 29; (20) De Lombaerde, cited above, p. 191; (21) De Lombaerde, cited above, p. 191. See also: *Bulletin*, July 1926, p. 197; (22) *The Work of Vocations at La Salette*, p. 43; (23) lbidem, p. 98; (24) *The Work of Vocations at La Salette*, new edition, augmented, 1887, p. 95; (25) Ibidem, p. 95; (26) Ibidem, p. 34. Read the whole 4th chapter on Bishop Fava's first visit to the School; (27) Ibidem, p. 37; (28) Ibidem, p. 77; (29) Ibidem, p. 79. Read all the tenth chapter devoted to the departure for Norway; (30) Ibidem, p. 79; (31) Ibidem, p. 80; (32) De Lombaerde, cited above, p. 196; (33) To read in the various issues of the *Bulletin* of 1926 some well-researched and interesting articles which Fr. Charles Rahier devoted to the Apostolic School on the occasion of his 50th-year jubilee; (34) *The Work of Vocations at La Salette*, 1884 edition, p. 97; (35) Ibidem, p. 9; (36) Ibidem, p. 86.

6
First Threats of Anticlericalism

Hardly had the school come into existence when it was threatened with extinction; thanks to the endeavors of Fr. Berthier, it proved to be strong enough to withstand the onslaughts of the enemy and imminent death. The infamous decrees of Jules Ferry, which presaged and tried to bring about the expulsion of all religious, soon menaced and threatened the young recruits of Saint-Joseph.

One can well imagine the alarm of the good Father and his children; this is easily detected in his little book which gives an account of events happening in the early years of the school.

Jules Ferry (1832-1898), a French statesman, promoter of secularism and colonial expansion

One of the students hearing this talk about expulsion said: "If they are going to drive us away, it would be better to put us to death than to cast us out into the world." (1)

These words and thousands like them dictated the policy of the Superiors; after the example of Saint Joseph under whose protection they had placed the school, they readied themselves to cross the frontier, leading their children into a more hospitable land to avoid perishing under the blows of these new Herods.

Fr. Berthier would have been among the first to adopt the password "death rather than life in the world"; under the present circumstances however, he would preferably chose exile to death because he wanted, above all things, to live as Christ did and for Christ, to carry on with the help of the Blessed Virgin and for the Blessed Virgin and ultimately establish a lasting apostolate.

The Commander-in-chief, Fr. Archier, after carefully scanning the horizon, sent his scouts into Switzerland in search of new camping grounds for the young soldiers of his first lieutenant, Fr. Berthier. The oldest would be sent there first and, if necessary, the rest of the troops would follow.

The oldest, that is the novices, were the first students who had taken the habit on the Holy Mountain on June 21, 1880. After wearing the cassock for six months, they laid aside the holy habit and returned to Saint-Joseph to complete their novitiate in lay dress, hoping in this manner to foil the investigations of the police. They were twelve, as were the apostles, and they enjoyed very much living with their younger brothers; they were however in constant fear of receiving orders to leave immediately.

Fr. Berthier was ever on the alert and there were many false alarms. It seems that one order to close the school had come as far as La Salette; a friend of the residence, the chief of police no doubt who was very devoted to the Fathers, either substituted other orders or had them cancelled. **(2)**

At any rate everyone was ready to leave at the first sign of danger. The novices went back to the Holy Mountain to make their profession on June 21, 1881, and again put aside the clerical garb.

A Scholasticate in Switzerland

Meanwhile a suitable house had been found in Switzerland and the General Council of the Institute had decided to send the newly professed and Fr. Berthier there to establish a Scholasticate. Thanks to Bishop Fava, who had, no doubt, intervened in higher places, the Apostolic School at Saint-Joseph remained open as well as that of Grenoble which had started in 1879. The present storm subsided somewhat because many religious were leaving or had left for Switzerland and the Missionaries, because they were missionaries, were allowed by the Bishop to continue their recruiting in France.

"In October 1881", relates Fr. Berthier without alluding to the persecution tactics of the government, "acting on the advice of Bishop Fava, Ordinary of Grenoble, we settled a group of our young men in a quiet Swiss valley; we had leased there at very moderate rates the mansion of the Baron of Werra, an adjacent farm and much surrounding land.

This house is admirably suited for serious study; it is located at La Souste, near Loeche in Valais, a delightful valley through which flows the river Rhine; (3) it is surrounded on all sides by beautiful high mountains. The residents are mostly Catholic and speak German.

The pioneers who were to settle in this valley left the Mountain and Saint-Joseph on October 15, 1881, to the tunes of farewell songs and amid the tears of their confreres. (4)

Thirteen students they were in all, eight of whom had just made their profession, five had taken their vows the previous year. They ran into all sorts of experiences on this journey – some comic, others tragic. Just before reaching Grenoble, their horses took fright as they were crossing the bridge, "Pont-de-Claix", and they almost ended up in the River Drac.

At Grenoble they experienced quite a bit of difficulty in dispatching a wagon load of baggage and furniture to Switzerland; even the police investigated under the pretext that the wagon ... was loaded with munitions for the enemy!

Fr. Berthier, escorted by two husky scholastics, went ahead and these three were the first to arrive in Geneva. Here again they experienced a bit of difficulty in shipping their wagon and supplies; Fr. Berthier was a bit scared as he walked through the streets of "the Protestant Rome" wearing his cassock. Fortunately he was flanked by two powerful protectors.

Two elderly ladies, benefactresses of the school, who had recently lost their brother, came to the rescue and outfitted them with lay garments; they put these on at the hotel and the next morning, on meeting the rest of the group at the railroad station, they were unrecognized for a while by their brothers. Everyone got a great laugh out of this picture, especially on seeing their Superior, defrocked and transformed into a Protestant minister.

The next day, October 23, a Saturday, they were on the move again, experiencing no further trouble and arrived safe and sound after visiting the Field of Agaunum where the Theban legion had shed its blood for Christ. The Salettine legion was to suffer great inconveniences from the severe Winter climate as well as many other privations, all of which would prepare them well for their future missionary life.

Life at La Souste

France was on the point of exiling all religious; would Switzerland be willing to receive them? As it had enacted laws to exclude them, would it be prudent to seek hospitality there?

Fr. Berthier asked himself this question and many others as he considered the possibility of trouble in this foreign land. True, this canton was Catholic; what encouraged him most was the fact that the head of the State Council was a prominent Catholic, whose zeal was in keeping with his faith.

Mr. Lucien Roten had been of invaluable assistance to many religious – the Jesuits, the Dominicans and the Redemptorists who had located temporarily in his canton. He gave the La Salette exiles a hearty reception and included them among those who enjoyed his protection and favors. He intervened with the Federal Council of Berne to mitigate the persecution laws and there have come down to us many excellent and courageous letters (5) which he wrote in defense of his administration which was taking care of those whom he had been happy and proud to welcome.

The Chateau Verrat, a La Salette residence from 1880 to 1896, was rented in La Souste, near Loèche in southwestern Switzerland

Fr. Berthier had a good friend and contact in Mr. Roten and placed his small colony under the protection of this beloved president. The police made many unexpected raids on La Souste on orders from the Federal Council of Berne but the agents of Mr. Roten had previously warned "the gentlemen of La Souste" so that when the police arrived they usually were found in their working clothes, toiling in the fields of their large farm. They seemed to be anything but fanatics and were very much like other poor devils of this region who were earning their bread at the sweat of their brow.

There were many close calls and once these were a thing of the past, there usually was much merriment; they also received many threats, none of which ever materialized. Thanks to the skill and diplomacy of Mr. Roten and also to the courage and work of "the gentlemen of La Souste", they were never in any serious or immediate danger and the students went on with their philosophical and theological studies in the guise of poor agricultural laborers.

On March 11, 1882, Mr. Roten wrote as follows to Fr. Berthier to set him at ease; "I am happy to inform you that it will be sufficient for you to bring your birth certificate to the Department of Justice and Police in order to obtain a permit to remain in the country. Your students will also have to obtain this permit from our department; to do so they will have to show their passport or other identification papers.

"I am making use of this opportunity to thank you for your charming letter; I appreciate it all the more because of the fact that one usually does not make friends by fulfilling one's duty. Man must have the courage of his convictions and the Council of State was happy to stand behind you on that occasion. In defending you, we defended the most precious heritage of our fathers, faith and freedom." **(6)**

The petition for permission to remain in the country had been forwarded to the Central Government and no answer seemed to be forthcoming. "It could be that justice has triumphed over political passion", conjectured the eminent head of the State; "I have great confidence in the majority of the members of our federal authority. Whatever be the decision of the Federal Council, I want to thank you in behalf of all the members of my State Council for your expressions of friendship. I am particularly grateful to you for your kind prayers as without God's blessing we are unable to accomplish anything, even though we have the best intentions in the world of doing our best for the happiness of those who have placed their confidence in us. The good relations I have had with many ecclesiastics, victims of persecution and fleeing from a country, which at one time was the glory of Christianity, will always stand out as a most precious memory of my administration as head of this State." (7)

The sword of Damocles was always hanging over us; at any moment a strict order from Berne could drive every religious community out of Switzerland. The Dominicans who were more conspicuous than the others and who were looked upon with a very evil eye by the Protestants of Berne decided to leave Sierre at the end of July 1883 and go to Holland.

"The regretted departure of our beloved neighbors", we read in the Annals of the residence of La Souste, "led us to believe that the Federal Council, satisfied by this move, would not disturb us in the future. Our Superior, Very Rev. Fr. Berthier, in the hope of bolstering our confidence, wrote to Mr. Roten, former President of the Government and now a member of the State Council at Sion. He received from him the following most reassuring reply." (8)

"Thank you for your souvenir; I accept it as another proof of a friendship most dear to me . . . I am also happy to inform you that the Federal Council has not made the least mention of your residence recently and that the addition of a few more students, to my mind, will make no difference. You can still rely on the assistance of your old friends, should any unexpected difficulty arise." (9)

It appeared that the little colony from now on would be able to enjoy many peaceful and productive years.

Heroic Pioneer Days

These beginnings were very, very difficult; those who experienced them refer to them as "the heroic days." Among other things, they had to repair and maintain a broken down mansion and cultivate 24 hectares of fallow land. They were blessed with strong arms and industrious good will; no one spared himself even in temperatures often 25 degrees below freezing. The food was poor and their living quarters most uncomfortable, yet that made no difference.

"The poor do not always have things to their liking", the Superior often repeated, "and as little as we have, we are much better off than was the Holy Family in Egypt." **(10)**

Fr. Berthier himself set the example in manual labor; in the evening he would peel the potatoes for the next day's soup; at other times he would help in the kitchen, plow the fields, do carpentry work or any other type of manual labor that had to be done. He and his assistants, that is, the students and professors, always reaped a rather good crop.

Flight into Egypt by **Albrecht Dürer (1494-1497)**

He was proud of their devotion to work which was modeled after his own; "Do you see that Father out there plowing the field? He is our philosophy professor", he said to a woman visitor. "Do not be surprised if our students labor in the fields; they were raised on farms and this work agrees with them very much. Besides, they are to be missionaries and a missionary must be able to take care of himself; it is a good thing for them to go through a period of apprenticeship." **(11)**

The Workers

As time went on, their number increased and Fr. Berthier, the master of all trades, organized them into many working groups; there were masons, painters, carpenters, binders and shoemakers who worked indoors; the outdoor work was taken care of by the gardeners, the tillers, the fishermen and bee-keepers. The elite group was the printers who operated the printing press which had been installed by Fr. Berthier for the purpose of publishing his writings.

The Director set his hand to everything; his favorite tool however was the pen. After giving his working orders for the day, he devoted himself to writing theology books and ascetic treatises. He always applied himself wholeheartedly and with his instinctive energy to everything he undertook, whether it was manual labor, the ministry of souls or intellectual work.

During the early months of the foundation, he was professor of philosophy and theology; when he was given two helpers, Fathers Besson and Rhoner who both were priests when they entered the Institute. He handed over to them these teaching assignments; he visited the classes often, assisted at the debates of the students, helped them in their difficulties and encouraged the scholastics and their teachers.

Swiss Apostolic School

"During the year 1883", writes a chronicler of that time – Fr. Berthier himself – "the thought came to us of establishing an Apostolic School in Switzerland, at La Souste." Authorization to do so was sought from the Bishop of Sion and the civil authorities of Valais. The bishop, who had been previously consulted, advised us to go on with our plans. Mr. Roten also was most encouraging and said that he in person would present our petition to the Council of State." **(12)**

Fr. Berthier had another enterprise on his hands and the new worries that came along with it. He took the necessary steps with the diocesan and civil authorities of the region and with the General Council of the Institute of which he was a member. After much insisting and some delay, authorization to proceed was finally given to him at a meeting of the Council held in January 1884; the Council of State approved the project on April 18, of the same year.

He immediately got to work, set his school in quarters apart from the Scholastlcate so as not to interfere in any way with its normal operation and then launched an appeal for vocations from the Valais. The response was very good. The immediate direction of the school was given to one of the older scholastics who had a good knowledge of German. On opening day in October, there were twelve students; later on they numbered 75. Fr. Berthier personally organized everything and carefully saw to it that these two parallel works, the German school and the French Scholasticate, got along smoothly.

One of these first Swiss Apostolics, one who was to be of great service to the Institute later on wrote as follows (13), "personally I hardly knew Fr. Berthier; true, he received me at the school of La Souste where I spent a year and a half as an apostolic; the scholastics were always in more immediate contact with him and therefore knew him more intimately.

"What impressed us about him was his piety, his great spirit of faith, his capacity for work, his ability to maintain a fine religious spirit in his large Salettine family; he always managed to make us feel happy in spite of the hard work we had to do and the numerous privations we suffered owing to circumstances. Modern comforts and conveniences are not a source of real happiness." (14)

First Ordinations

"On June 3, 1884", we read in the Annals of the residence, "there was held the greatest celebration ever in our community, for on that day there took place the ordination of the three first priests out of the apostolic school of Our Lady of La Salette; on that same day, eight received the diaconate and seventeen the minor orders. Never in the history of the congregation had such a large group of her children advanced in the hierarchical orders of the church." (15)

"These were all Fr. Berthier's and Fr. Archier's children; the latter had come from the Holy Mountain to attend the ordinations and take part

Bishop Adrian Jardinier (1808-1901), Ordinary of Sion, Switzerland

in the festivities. Bishop Jardinier, Ordinary of Sion, who had always been most friendly to us since his first visit to La Souste in December, 1881, most obligingly came to the Scholasticate for the ordination ceremonies.

Mr. Roten, a sincere friend of the community in its earliest days, had planned to attend the festivities; unable to do so he however made a brief appearance at the end of the banquet which followed the ordinations and received a long and warm ovation. Our chronicler remarks that, at his arrival, when they no longer expected him, our joy was complete; everyone in the gathering broke out in songs honoring the Bishop and the brave statesman, known as the protector of exiled religious." (16)

Fr. Berthier had organized the feast with his usual ability; he kept in the background however to give all possible prominence to his illustrious guests.

His children were always grateful for his devotion to them and they expressed their appreciation on days such as the New Year and St. John's Day which was his feast day. His silver jubilee was celebrated October 16, 1887, and the diarist of that day records the events in rather enthusiastic prose.

"What a wonderful day", says he, "was the 16th of October when we celebrated the 25th anniversary of our beloved Father! On the 20th of September of this year he completed twenty-five years in the priesthood. What a joy it was for all his children to express their gratitude and love! God grant that he remain a long time among us! The festivities of that day were heightened by the first communion of three of our Apostolics and the opening of our new chapel which was blessed in the morning by Fr. Berthier with the permission of Bishop Jardinier." (17)

Trip to Rome

This wish of the chronicler (which was also that of the entire community) did not prevent this apostolic man from resuming the full time work of preaching missions. Before laying aside his charge, he had the happiness of taking a trip to Rome in April, 1888; at that time he accompanied Fr. Archier, the Superior General, to convey to Leo XIII (1810-1903), on the occasion of his sacerdotal jubilee, the wishes, the prayers, the great love and eternal gratitude of the Congregation and of each of its members to the Holy See." A modest offering was presented to the Holy Father along with these wishes."

"While in Rome, they discussed many questions of great importance to the future of the community", writes the chronicler. "They made a pilgrimage to Loretto and Assisi. Our beloved Superior returned here the evening of April 23. He gave us several conferences on his trip at chapel in the evening, all of which helped to increase in our hearts the great love we already had for the capital of the Christian world and its illustrious leader." **(18)**

Absences and Departure from La Souste

He would often hand over the reins of office to competent assistants and this allowed him to absent himself to work at his beloved apostolic delight of preaching missions. He would go back every year to the Holy Mountain when the beautiful weather had set in to devote himself to the ministry of preaching and hearing confessions. In Winter he often went into France to preach missions in one diocese or another. Our chronicler follows him very carefully on these

Basilica of Our Lady of Fourvières, in Lyon, France

journeys and he makes special mention of the great happiness Fr. Berthier experienced when he took along with him the first priests who had come out of his dear apostolic school on their first mission.

"Fr. Berthier left April 7", notes our chronicler, "accompanied by two young priests, Frs. Vernet and François Comte, to conduct a mission at Benost, in the Diocese of Belley (France). Let us remark in passing that this was the first attack launched against the gates of hell and the world by the students of the Apostolic School of Our Lady of La Salette. After their mission, they went to Fourvières to replenish their strength at the feet of her who is the Tower of David; they then proceeded to La Salette, a spot that held such fond memories for them." (19)

Fr. Berthier was happy to supervise and assist his first fledglings in their initial apostolic flights.

He lost no time in coming down to the rank of private soldier in the army of the Missionaries of La Salette and in joining them in their many difficult tasks. His health was better than ever and he had lost none of his ardor during the quiet years he spent training youngsters for the missionary priesthood.

On December 2, 1888, he resigned his office of Superior; a few months later, on April 24, 1889, he gave up the directorship of the Apostolic School of La Souste.

And so it was that, as he was approaching his fiftieth year, he laid aside the work he had done so well at the school to take up again the apostolate of preaching missions which had always been his life's ambition and to go forth again, as he had done in his youth, to battle against the enemies of Christ, his Lord and Master.

Endnotes

(1) *The Work of Vocations at La Salette*, p. 67; (2) Several information and details of this paragraph were provided by two novices of that time: Fr. Jean Maron, M.S. (1857-1930) who became superior of La Souste after Fr. Berthier and Fr. Louis Comte, M.S. (1860-1934), who was to found, after another persecution, that of Combes, in 1901, La Salette of Tournai in Belgium. See also as derived from the same source of information, the article of Fr. Charles Rahier, M.S. (1898-1969), *on the Residence of La Souste Near Loèche in Valais* in the *Bulletin* of October 1926, p. 310-314; (3) *The Work of Vocations at La Salette*, 1884 edition, p. 94; (4) Ibidem; (5) See them at the beginning of the *Annals of the House of Loèche in Valais*, Archives of the Institute; (6) *Annals of the House of Loèche*; (7) Ibidem; (8) Ibidem; (9) Ibidem; (10) De Lombaerde, cited above, p. 283; (11) Unpublished letter to Miss Laurentine Deschaux. The worker has become an excellent Missionary of La Salette in Brazil. (12) *Annals of the Loèche Mission*. Year 1883; (13) Fr. Charles Grenat, M.S. (1870-1952), who was a long-time teacher of theology at the Scholasticate at Rome, then General Counselor and Superior of the House of Tournai during the Great War 1914-1918; (14) Letter to the author, written from Grenoble, February 18th, 1929; (15) *Annals*, Year 1884; (16) Ibidem; (17) *Annals*, Year 1887; (l8) *Annals*, Year 1888; (19) *Annals*, Year 1886.

7
The Popular Writings of Fr. Berthier

The spoken apostolate and that of the written word are in the case of Fr. Berthier a manifestation of two aspects of that great missionary activity of his which kept renewing itself and increasing in him as he advanced in age. They are, as it were, two poles around which his whole life revolve. He was born to write and he was born to preach; his writings will give longer life to his voice and his books will reecho his numberless sermons.

Archbishop François de Salignac de la Mothe-Fénelon (1651-1715)

The silent word which flows from his pen into the intimate depths of the soul are no less pleasing and helpful than the eloquent word which he speaks from the pulpit.

Let us add that the eloquence of this apostolate of his is based on the simplicity of his word and style. Unknown to himself young Berthier was learning the art of writing in a book entitled "*Telemachus*" which his father had given him to read, one about which he later on said much evil because the gods and goddesses who conversed with humans and influenced their minds could have turned away his tender and candid soul from the true God as his little mind at the time was unable to reconcile their senseless talk with the teachings of his catechism. (1)

The colorless style of Archbishop François Fénelon (1651-1715) characterizes the writings of Fr. Berthier; the sentences of Fr. Sylvan-Marie Giraud, M.S., rise to great heights after the manner of Bp. Jacques-Bénigne Bossuet (1627-1704), those of Fr. Berthier are rather down to earth, and deliberately so, and thus assume the nonchalance of Fénelon.

He learned to write chiefly at the school of Our Lady of La Salette, borrowing from her a manner of expression that has in it nothing of inane verbalism and affectation; it is a style that appeals directly to the people, one that states facts plainly, without subtle and excessive use of words.

He writes as follows in his book: "*The Marvels of La Salette*": "To extoll these marvels adequately one would need the eloquence of an orator, the inspiration of a poet and the brush of a most skilled painter."

"Experience, however, teaches us that truth presented without varnish has its charms and its perfume. The lowly violet in the flower bed has not the brilliance of the rose yet it will delight the heart of him who picks it; all songbirds are not nightingales yet they all sing the praises of him who created them. Mary too can expect to be blessed and praised by all types of voice."

"That is why we have written, in our own simple way, about the wonders of the Apparition of September 19, 1846." **(2)**

His writing style imitated Mary's manner of speaking. He uses it not only to sing the praises of this Virgin but also to have her "praised and blessed by everyone." He makes use of it to repeat Mary's message to the whole Christian world and we find it in everyone of his works; it is productive of results and most appealing to the average person.

Since Fr. Berthier addresses his words to the common people, as did the Blessed Virgin, his style is that of the people; so also is the eloquence of his sermons when he preaches. He makes every effort to use simple and at times even dull language although on occasion, as often happens with average folks, his words will flow in rich and spontaneous outbursts. As a rule, he does not seek literary effect.

Those who have known him have consistently claimed that he could have been outstanding, even among the best; but vainglory was not part of his makeup. He made it a point to remain at the level of the average man because he wanted to attract him to Mary and lead him back to Our Lord, ever mindful of the fact that Mary and her Son spoke the language of the common people.

This popular style comes more easily to him when he speaks than when he writes; writing seems to bore him and for that reason he speaks or talks in his writings. The pen cools his ardor, lessens his enthusiasm and deadens the animation of this thoughts.

He was all fire and flame in the pulpit, at times rising to brilliant heights; at other times remaining calm and collected. I heard him speak only once at La Salette; the extraordinary thing I remarked about him was that he appeared fiery and collected at one and the same time. He spoke with his eyes closed almost all the time and when he opened them, he seemed to penetrate to the very depths of my soul as a novice.

Writing takes away from the spontaneity of his lively and mobile nature, but he tries to compensate for this by writing in a speaking style, talking the language of the people; he uses all possible means to interest the indifferent reader and to hold the attention of the distracted one.

"Long works are no longer read nowadays", he admits sadly in the conclusion of his book; "*The Marvels of La Salette*"; neither are lengthy sermons appreciated. (3) We can honestly say, in reference to Fr. Berthier's books, that they are all practically brief allocutions, lively homilies, a succession of short exhortations, all of which afford no time for the reader to fall asleep.

His writings have a strong sermon tone; he considered his sermons as acts in a play and when he wrote he visualized an audience listening to him. Here is a remark he makes at the beginning of one of his books: (4) "Many times have I seen audiences moved to tears as they listened to certain incidents I am publishing in this book." he had given so many missions and retreats that his audiences were con-

LES MERVEILLES

DE

LA SALETTE

PAR

L'abbé J. BERTHIER, M. S.

> Eh bien! mes enfants, vous le ferez passer à tout mon peuple.
> (*Paroles de N.-D. de la Salette.*)

PARIS
ANCIENNE MAISON CHARLES DOUNIOL
P. TÉQUI, SUCCESSEUR
29, *rue de Tournon*, 29
—
1898

Fr. Berthier's, *The Marvels of La Salette*, **published in 1898**

stantly before his eyes; his books are sermons to young girls, Christian mothers, men, children, priests and religious. All his writings, even those which treat historical subjects, have a catechetical tone and the charm of childlike simplicity; this is also typical of his mission sermons.

He knows that the mind of the average person does not enjoy difficult abstractions and interminable dissertations; it needs little food but it must be the best. Its attention must be held; it must be aroused and renewed continually; it must be given time to pause and rest; unbridled oratory would surely put it to sleep.

All Fr. Berthier's works are light and lightsome; none of them are tiresome, neither do they require much effort on the part of the reader to follow the development of any question. Every book has clear-cut divisions and subdivisions, number after number' to mark out each paragraph.

It is easy enough to criticize this system for want of anything else with which to find fault. To understand why he used it, one must call to mind the special group of people to whom he directed his writings; namely, those who have hardly any time to read or are unable to read much at a time. The author has the ideal method which is most suitable to the average working man since it does not take away from his working day nor does it interfere with his distractions and necessary relaxation.

When he writes for priests, he wants to offer those "who are much taken up with the work of the ministry an easy means of calling back to memory the most important notions of the various branches of sacred science." He does his best "in a 600-page book, two columns per page, fine printing and easy to read" to summarize the most important points of Moral and Dogmatic Theology, Canon Law, Liturgy and Philosophy – and there are more than 2,790 numbered sections. "Reviewing two pages of this summary a day", he says, "would enable you to go over your whole seminary course in one year." (5)

As regards his skill in the "art of transition", we can compare him to Nicholas Boileau (1636-1711) in *Art Poétique (poetic art)*; he has none. After saying one thing, he simply goes to say another. He figures that the commonplace reader might get lost should things become a bit complicated.

He leads the reader from a quotation to a text, from an example taken from history to a moral counsel, without rhetorical formula or hidden connection but with sincerity and directness.

He aims to be brief so as not to tire the reader and he does his utmost to hold his attention by some striking image, an interesting sentence or the beauty of some historical event. His technique is identical to that which he uses in the pulpit; that is, he is practical, realistic, "having in mind the success of his ministry and the good of souls."

Writing in reference to one of his books, he makes the following statement **(6)**: "There is nothing like stories to make a sermon interesting and to hold the attention of the listeners; people lire nothing better. The easiest way to move and inspire them with generous sentiments is to set before them, not great ideas but great examples and model. A short lesson is quickly understood when we see it put into execution practically under our very eyes." **(7)**

Stained glass window of the Holy Family

His books are replete with quotations. We can even say that his written work is made up of quotation marks within which he inserts the best of his readings, beautiful maxims, striking examples, events and quests of history along with moral counsels and solid theological doctrine. These quotations are so many jewels mounted on a background of copper or brass; his style is the poor metal encompassing the precious stones.

The quotations from numberless authors are taken from everyone and everywhere. He must be given credit for being able to insert them in their proper setting; before doing this, he had to select the appropriate quotation from an enormous collection of documents which he had at hand. These selections had previously been taken down as notes from spiritual authors, whether patristic or ascetic, theological or moral.

Once this has ben done he retires, as it were into the background; what then stands out is the doctrine of the doctors and saints of the Church. He does not have time to examine thoroughly, to synthesize and discuss at any length their complete teaching, but he does have the genius to extract the best of what they wrote, to express their thoughts clearly and place them in the hands of the faithful.

His literary work is analogous to his hobby of collecting herbs and flowers, one he enjoyed so much while at La Salette and La Souste. His books are "herbaria" in which is displayed a variety of flowers, namely, quotations and stories to be enjoyed by the young and the old. "In presenting these to the public", he is confident, "that they will spread in the hearts of all the odor of truth and virtue." **(8)**

People enjoy collections, albums, especially pictures and flowers. Fr. Berthier has a great variety of these in the shape of quotations and stories, at a very moderate price too, all of which are able to satisfy the yearnings of the human heart and comfort the interested soul.

"We are living in a day", says he, "when individuals are unable to concentrate for any length of time on anything serious; we must therefore speak to them in short sentences and hold their attention with stories; also must we avoid keeping them too long a time on the same subject or tiring them with too symmetrical a plan." **(9)**

The use of this method in writing a book is little complicated and it appealed very much to Fr. Berthier. Writing was a pleasant interlude between Missions and other pressing duties as well as a means of extending his apostolate to those his sermons could not reach; even as a young priest, he dreamed of becoming a writer and he mentioned this to his old friend, the pastor of Veyssilieu, stating at the time that he would like "to publish a manual for Christian girls or something of that nature."

On November 12, 1865, he wrote him as follows: "How about giving me a helping hand? In your charity, please take down a few notes for me in a copy book, anything you might run across that could have some connection with my subject, especially matter from the lives of the saints. Do that in the Winter time and send me what you have in the Spring; this will be a distraction for you and at the same time you will contribute to a good work. These notes do not have to be numbered or in order; many a good hook has come out of pell-mell notes." (10)

In his literary apostolate, he keeps to a minimum any personal contribution; he relies on the best in Christian tradition in his quest for stray souls. He glories in this and even makes it a point to see that the ideas expressed in his writings are not his own.

"Our doctrine is not our own", he dares to say with Our Blessed Lord, "but that of the Sacred Scriptures, the Fathers of the Church and the theologians." (11)

"We have put together", says he at the beginning of another book, "what we have found in the writings of the Fathers, theological authors and other reputable writers, to be most able to edify. We make it a point", he said as though making a Profession of Faith, "to say nothing of our own on the beautiful and sublime subjects which we treat." (12)

Bookcase with chained book from the library of Cesena, Italy; artist: engraving by John Willis Clark (1833–1910)

"Our reason for this procedure is that it is much better to base our judgment and our manner of acting on the teachings of those who are our masters and guides than to follow the venturous path laid out by so-called experience or personal ideas." (13)

When discussing "vocations", a meet difficult subject and one which

79

has always given rise to interminable arguments, Fr. Berthier has no intention of entering into any controversy on the subject "by condemning certain theories which are quite prevalent in our day and also quite contrary to right doctrine"; neither does he attempt to persuade anyone to enter this or that state of life. We simply want to set forth in print what appears to us to be the truth", he says categorically. (14)

He always considered it most useful "to make serious researches into the writings of the great masters and teachers and gather their teachings in one volume which could be read by everyone." (15)

His entire written work is an extract, "a conscientious exposé" of Christian doctrine taken from his favorite authors. In his book on *The Various States of the Christian Life and Vocation according to the Teaching of the Doctors of the Church and Theologians*, he lists the names of his favorite authors who are a source of inspiration to him and whose writings form the texture of all his works; thus it was that he could truly say that his doctrine was not his own but that of the Church, explained, commented upon, developed and defended by the greatest geniuses of Christianity.

He cites the Doctors of the Church, especially St. John Chrysostom, Saint Jerome, Saint Augustine, Saint Thomas Aquinas, Saint Alphonsus Ligouri, Francisco Suárez, Thomas Sanchez, Leonardus Lessius, S.J., Saint Ignatius Loyola and finally Fr. John Peter Pinamonti; "there you have my sources", he says without shame or fear of being called a plagiarist. "They are rich and we here drawn abundantly from them, more so in this particular case where the matter treated is of such great importance that we did not wish to say anything on our own authority." (16)

His citations are numerous in every one of his works and each of these contributes to a literary ensemble based on solid doctrine; all reference sources are clearly indicated. As he says himself: "Everyone will be able to verify the exactness of our quotations because we have scrupulously pointed out the sources from which they have been taken." **(17)**

When referring to the translation of some of his citations he makes the following remark: "We do not give a word for word translation of the Fathers and theologians; what we try to do is to give an exact exposition of their doctrine." **(18)**

His first biographer, Fr. de Lombaerde says of Fr. Berthier that his books are "a proof of Fr. Berthier's great caution and a fruit of deep study of the sacred writers and the Fathers. His works are a reproduction, a coordination, a sort of concordance of the teachings of the Fathers and the saints; everything is taken from them. To attack the writings of this holy priest would be to attack the Fathers, the Doctors of the Church, the Church itself whose words he quotes in proof of every one of his statements. We daresay "Every one of his statements" because we firmly believe that every assertion he ever made could have been substantiated by something he had read in approved teachers, especially in the writings of the saints." **(19)**

He always kept in mind the example of Our Lady of La Salette and pondered on the tone and import of her discourse of September 19, 1846. There was nothing new, nothing original or pretentious about the contents of her message. She was humbly satisfied – call to mind the *Magnificat*, that beautiful chain of texts borrowed from Holy Scripture – yes, she was humbly satisfied to remind men of the Lord's Decalogue which they had forgotten, of the teachings of her Divine Son whom they scorned; she also insisted on the practices of religion.

Dogma and moral – the whole of Christian teaching – are the subjects of Fr. Berthier's eloquent simplicity, just as these were the topics of Mary's conversation at La Salette. He instructs the average person in the elementary truths of Christianity; his works are catechisms enlarged and developed, even catechisms with pictures and examples. When he writes for elite souls, his books contain the precise rules and elevated truths of the religious life or of the priesthood.

We can truly say of his writings what he himself said of the discourse of Our Lady of La Salette: "It is an utterance that has much substance, just like the Gospels. It contains a summary of the commandments of God and of the Church, of the divine law and of Catholic doctrine. It is an epitome of evangelical morality." **(20)**

The title of one of his books (it was in print out a short time and now is not to be found anywhere) explains, as it were, his purpose in writing and the reason why he wrote in the manner he did; The book is entitled: *Le Fidèle et l'âme religieuse éclairés sur les vérités de la foi et les devoirs de la vie chrétienne et de la vie parfait* (*The Faithful and Religious soul enlightened on the truths and duties of the Christian and Perfect Life*).

Fr. Giraud enlightened the "faithful and religious soul" on one particular point which he had very much at heart; that is, the spirit of sacrifice and the life of victim. Fr. Berthier had no special or preferred teaching to expound; his one main objective was to explain every point of Christian and religious doctrine so as to enlighten everyone especially the indifferent and the ignorant, with the light of truth.

With this end in view he wrote so many easy-to-understand and impersonal books that his written work is a veritable encyclopedia. It is a *Summa*, the product of intense work; It is a *Summa* of religion but one that is easily understood by the mass of the people and, to use the title of one of his books, it is *Le Livre de Tous* (*The Book for All*). It is a *Summa* of sound Christian common sense, unadulterated by strange ideas and bizarre practices.

Since the above comparison brings to mind the work of Saint Thomas Aquinas, it must be said that Fr. Berthier was a great admirer of his. It has been said, not without a great deal

Fr. Berthier's, *The Book for All*, 1901

of exaggeration, that St. Thomas lives again in the writings of this holy priest and manifests in the letter's writings the full depth of his genius. **(21)** He borrowed from the saint his method of divisions and subdivisions; these, at first glance, appear dry but they are most practical and effective in impressing truths on the mind of the average person.

To give you one example among thousands, here is how he outlines his *Study of the Religious Life*. "After speaking briefly about its origin, its excellence and its advantages, we will consider whether it is a matter of precept or of counsel and if it is allowed for one to make a vow of entering it. We will then ask ourselves if it is permitted to exhort others to enter religion and if it is forbidden to deter them from becoming religious; finally, we will examine the principal impediments to entering this state of life and solve a few questions connected with this subject." **(22)**

"And on all these points, he's very careful to add, we do not say nothing that relies on the authority of the Doctors and Theologians most esteemed."

This strict impersonality is conducive "to great exactness in doctrine" **(23)** and gives him access to an abundance of important matter. He is able to condense the contents of several folio books into one of his smaller volumes. He says somewhere **(24)** that he once used the summaries of 30 volumes to compose one of his own books. He refers to one of his books **(25)** as "a dictionary of texts"; a certain bishop used to call him a "living library of priestly science." **(26)**

The tireless and monumental work of Father Berthier resembles that of Saint Jerome whose he loved to highlight the amazing literary activity and of which he said that having read everything, he was picking up, so to speak, in himself the testimony of all the others and that of the universal tradition." **(27)**

Endnotes

(1) De Lombaerde, *Life of Fr. Berthier*, p. 29; (2) *The Wonders of La Salette*, Téqui, Paris (1898); (3) Ibidem, p. 342; (4) *Words and historical features*, 1898 edition, p. 6; (5) *Propaganda Catalog*, 1896, p. 42. *Brief Compendium of Dogmatic and Moral Theology*, 1887; (6) *Words and remarkable historical traits*; (7) *Propaganda catalog*, p. 4; (8) *A garland of the most beautiful flowers. At the author's home at La Salette* (1892). Preface; (9) *The most remarkable words and historical treatises*. Lyon, Briguet (1898). Preface; (10) *Letters to the priest of Veyssilieu* (1865-1866). 7th Letter; (11) *The States of Christian Life*, Introduction, p. x; (12) *The Priesthood*, 1898 edition. Preface, p. 10; (13) *The States of Christian Life*, Introduction, p. xi.; (l4) Ibidem, p. x; (15) Ibidem, p. ix; (16) Ibidem, p. x; (17) Ibidem, p. xi ; (18) Ibidem, p. 1, note (1); (19) De Lombaerde, cited above, p. 321; (20) *Annals*, year 1867, p. 492, year 1877, p. 720; (21) De Lombaerde, cited above, p. 329; (22) *The States of Christian Life*, p. 84; (23) *The Priesthood*, p. 10; (24) Propaganda Prospectus, Year 1896, p. 5; (25) *Biblical Opinions and Examples*, see Propaganda brochure, p. 12; (26) De Lombaerde, cited above, p. 349; (27) *The States of Christian Life*, p. 7 (1896).

8
Promotion of Fr. Berthier's Books

Fr. Berthier's written work has the mark of universality; it discusses everything contained in Christian teaching and it was intended for everybody: we can refer to it as "a compendium of theology for the mass (1) of the people", a term which he used in advertising his favorite works, "*The Book for All*."

For these books to be productive of good everywhere, they had, in the words of the Virgin of La Salette, "to be made known to *all* her people."

Hence his great desire of initiating an intensive advertising campaign to spread his books around and further his written apostolate. He was not the type who wrote for collectors of rare books, neither was he likely to have only a few copies printed, at an unheard of price, for the delight of book lovers as have done so many of our present day writers of logogriphs. He could not understand how a book could be published and read by no one, placed in a showcase, left to lie on a library shelf or hidden away in a closet. A book according to him is a missionary that must go far and wide for the glory of God and the salvation of souls.

Fr. Berthier had specialized in writing with clarity and simplicity so as to be read and understood by everybody; he made it a point also to devise the best possible means and ways of making himself known and, by so doing, reach as large as possible a number of readers. He organized and maintained a well conducted publicity campaign, not for the sake of financial gain but to accomplish practical and lasting good.

He understood as a very young writer the importance of winning readers. It hurt him very much to see that nothing was being done to promote the spread of the books of his own Superior, Fr. Giraud, and he was going to make sure that he would not be a victim of this same indifference. During most of his life, he had to contend with prejudice and petty misunderstandings as there were some who accused him of personal ambition, rashness and even of inefficiency. He clearly outlined his course and pursued it vigorously, advertising and selling his books everywhere.

He kept after his old Curé of Veyssilieu, imploring him to get down to serious business and do something about getting his first book before the public.

He wrote to him July 29, 1865, begging him not to let his book suffer the fate which had plagued the mystical Fr. Giraud's "*Vie d'Union*"; "the booksellers to whom you would entrust my book would advertise it, whereas here books seem to remain in their shipping cases; at Grenoble possibly three copies of Fr. Giraud's *Vie d'Union* are sold every two weeks." (2)

St. Thomas Aquinas, between Plato and Aristotle, triumphs over Averroes by Benozzo Gozzoli (1420–1497)

He always made it a point to contact the best Catholic publishers and booksellers of France, especially those in the larger cities. He dealt with Baratier and Dardelet of Grenoble, Josserand and Briguet of Lyons, Taffin-Lefort of Lille, Haton and Tequi of Paris and many others until he definitively did business with "La Bonne Presse" of Paris.

"Fr. Mussel", he says in the above quoted letter, "advises me to have my book printed in Paris and he remarks, with very good reason too, that the Pilgrimage is not a suitable place for the sale of books, especially when these do not deal exclusively with pious subjects." (3)

He writes as follows to the same correspondent on August 10, 1865:

> "In order to reach the greatest number of people possible, and in this particular case, a large number of Christian mothers, it would be a good idea to send copies to convent boarding schools for the opening of the scholastic year, so that the mothers who accompany their children to school might obtain a copy; we could interest Superiors and Directresses of other boarding schools by sending them complimentary copies." (4)

This was one little scheme he thought up to promote the sale of his first book; another good selling point would be the low price. "The copy printed on cheaper paper must not be too expensive ", he writes and, after fixing a minimum price, he continues as follows: "Our chief aim must be to do as much good as possible ... These good mothers must be made acquainted with their duties and I am confident that this little book, should it be read, will with God's blessing accomplish much good." (5)

Mothers of families were not the only ones for whom the zealous Missionary wrote; as time went on, he composed books for young men and young women, for children, for the entire family, for the priest and the religious, for every state of life and every type of Christian soul. His one ambition was to reach everybody by means of low priced small books.

Low priced books did not always appeal to publishers and booksellers who naturally had financial gain in view. Why not become a publisher and editor himself? Then the La Salette Scholasticate at Loeche had been established on a solid footing, he bought a printing press at a very reasonable price; he was now equipped to print a large number of his books at very low cost; the printing was done by the students of philosophy and theology and they turned out to be excellent printers.

Several of them who later on became priests and Missionaries often spoke of this work which they had been very happy to do. Only the best and most intelligent students were chosen for this work; among them there were compositors, readers, printers, folder„ typesetters and whatnot. They were not professionals but they did very good work printing several books of Fr. Berthier.

This equipment was far from the best; there was too much work, too little results in comparison to the energy and time expended. Besides this system worked too slowly to suit Fr. Berthier, the master compositor, whose manuscripts drove even the most active workers to despair. This project was given up even before they left Loeche.

At that time, in 1894, Fr. Berthier contacted the "Bonne Presse" of Paris and the job of reprinting almost all of Fr. Berthier's books, which by the way were widely read in Catholic circles, were given to this concern. The *Croix de Paris (Cross of Paris)* periodically invited its readers "to supply themselves with weapons of war from the Catholic arsenal of Fr. Berthier." **(6)** He called this "Croix" the greatest medium of religious publicity of our century; it is possible that there has been, nothing comparable to it, even in the past centuries. **(7)**

He later on resumed his printing activities and his spiritual sons of the Institute of the Holy Family took up this work in a very big way. In some of their residences, they have excellent modern printing presses with which the many and always modern works of their indefatigable Founder are printed in many languages.

His missions afforded him many opportunities for distributing brochures and outlines of his books; his annual sojourn on the Holy Mountain brought him into contact with many zealous women who devoted much of their time to propaganda work for his books.

It was during the last decade of the 1800s, specifically in 1894, that he undertook a most intensive and extensive campaign. Having obtained the approbation of Fr. Mussel, he announced his "Read Catholic Books" campaign by means of a prospectus which he inserted in every one of his books.

The Vicar General of Grenoble wrote as follows on September 15, 1894: "We approve the campaign for the spread of good books which is being launched by Fr. Berthier, Missionary of La Salette. His purpose is to place in every home, for the good of souls, useful and practical books. We draw this campaign to the attention of the clergy and religious communities and heartily recommend it to their zeal."

Very much encouraged by this cooperation of the chancery in

his effort to place a Catholic book in every home, "he contacted as many persons as he could and offered his collection of books for this purpose to his brothers in the priesthood, to the deans in the various dioceses, to the directors of minor seminaries and ecclesiastical colleges, to the Chaplains and Superiors of religious men and women, asking the priests to mention his books to their confreres, especially at ecclesiastical conferences; also requesting the Superiors of large communities to make his works known to the members of their different residences when they would at some time or other be gathered together on retreat.

He conceived the idea of supplying books to those who could give them as rewards and prizes. "This would be an effective way", he said, "of introducing useful books into the home and, at the same time, help in putting together a Catholic library." For this purpose, he provided books in all formats with deluxe bindings and beautifully illustrated. He was confident that he could compete with "a lot of useless books" which were good sellers because of their low prices the beauty of their format, of their illustrations and of their bindings. He would meet this competition not only with moderately low prices but also by means of "the thoroughly Christian atmosphere of his doctrinal and historical books" which he felt certain "he could sell at as low a price as anybody else."

In certain antichristian schools, books given as prizes are a means of perversion; why should we not make an apostolate of giving good ones as rewards?" **(8)**

I remember very well – that was in 1896, the year I entered the school at Joseph Chanrion Street in Grenoble – how much I used to marvel at the piles of books stacked in the basement room by which we used to pass three times a day on our way to the refectory. We used to cast an eager eye on the books which had such beautiful bindings and when we could get away from recreation, we made it a point to steal in and look through them, admiring the beautiful pictures. There was quite a stockpile of all kinds of books, some bound, others stitched and all written by Fr. Berthier.

I used to envy the brother in charge of these books; he was proud of his occupation and he used to scold us in no uncertain terms when he caught us browsing through these volumes. He spent most of the day, not reading them, but packing them in shipping cases which were expedited everywhere.

Fr. Berthier used to enjoy watching the good brother work; at times he would give him a helping hand, all the while cheering him on with jovial words and a winning smile.

Another student of those days, who often saw the brother and Fr. Berthier working together, relates the following: "I remember very well what the brother porter of the La Salette Fathers' residence at Grenoble, who was in charge of shipping the books, used to say to me: "that Fr. Berthier is causing quite a stir everywhere by the variety and number of his books." He also gave an example of how the good Father had him fill out a large order for one of his customers. Fr. Berthier preferably referred to his books, not by their title but rather by their contents or the group of persons for whom they were written. Here is an example of what the good brother packed in one case:

Fr. Berthier's, *The Religious State, its Excellence, Advantages, Obligations and Privileges*, published in 1893

> "We have a large order of books today, brother; be sure to pack them well. At the bottom of the case you will place my theology and Our Lady of La Salette; also include in that case many Mothers according to the mind of God, Man as he should be, a few Ideal Young Men, some Young Girls, some Priests and quite a number of Little Children; in the center

place, Our Lord Jesus Christ and the Virgin Mary. Don't forget the Priesthood and the Religious State; throw in a good number of Books For All. Don't forget Historical Traits, Vocations, Novenas and Sententiae. Cover the whole thing with a profusion of "Bouquet", "Garlands" and "Baskets" of most beautiful flowers!

This same correspondent who had lived many years as a Missionary, a great imitator of his model, Fr. Berthier, and just as active, writes as follows from the depths of his Carthusian Monastery solitude, where he had retired at the conclusion of his Missionary career:

> "The whole written work of Fr. Berthier is indeed a little university, a true mosaic, a complete library of spirituality. There is something in it for everyone; he wrote for all and wants to come into contact with the soul of every man." (9)

Did he attain this beautiful objective and reach this apostolic goal? It would be difficult to give an adequate answer. It seems certain however that Fr. Berthier brought back to Jesus Christ a greater number of souls than any other spiritual writer; it is very evident also that the books he wrote for the average person had a most popular appeal and were more widely read than other spiritual books.

His written work was placed in the hands of all and could be found in every library. His writings were never relegated to a forgotten spot; on the contrary, they were always close at hand like a faithful friend who is consulted in the hour of trail or at a time of great decision. His books, replete with prayers, seem more suitable for Church use where one meditates and pauses for a while than for the library, where one drops in for reference and then moves on.

His books have been a great help to individuals in their hour of need. They have made a deep impression on souls and have contributed much in spreading the good news of Christ's gospel and the message of his Mother.

Fr. Augustin Rivoire, whom I quoted in the preceding paragraphs, after finishing his studies in Rome, preached missions for many years in France and in America; he made the following remark in reference to the broad field of Fr. Berthier's apostolate:

> "I noticed that whenever the question of La Salette was brought up, whether in Rome or in America, it was always followed by another: 'Did you know Fr. Giraud and Fr. Berthier? Their books are widespread and well known; in fact, Fr. Berthier's reputation is due to his books."

It may be that no man is a prophet in his own country; neither is he properly appreciated there; Fr. Berthier however came into prominence here at home through the beautiful books he offered us and the great success they enjoyed. When I was a youngster at the Apostolic School, his books, bound in deluxe bindings, used to be awarded to us at the distribution of prizes. We had no difficulty at all in understanding their contents and we admired very much the beautiful illustrations they contained; later on it took us a full year, that of the Novitiate, to go through one book of Fr. Giraud's without understanding it any too well.

Fr. Berthier always succeeded in interesting young people; that does not mean that older persons were bored by his books; far from that. Priests also made good use of his writings.

Fr. Rivoire related the following: "I have found his books in many of the parish rectories when I was preaching missions in the United States. I used to sell *Le Livre de Tous (The Book for All)* in the sacristy, introducing this book into many homes as a means of continuing the mission and perpetuating its fruits. I did this same thing in the English-speaking parishes as the Sisters, the Faithful Companions of Jesus of Fitchburg, Massachusetts, had translated this book, *Le Livre de Tous* into English. We have no idea of how great a help to Missionaries and Pastors, here in Europe and on the missions, were his *Compendium Theologiae (Compendium of Theology)*, *The Priest*, *Historical Traits*, etc. ... I personally have used his books often and many of my confreres have made the following admission to me: "if you need a

Charterhouse of the Carthusian Monastery of Farneta, in Lucca, in the Tuscany area of central Italy

sermon in a hurry or want a quick solution to a case of conscience, go to Fr. Berthier; he will not let you down."

"In some of our Carthusian monasteries", adds the same correspondent, "his theology is in each cell and put to very good use. Here at the Chartreuse of Farneta, we have almost all his books. In 1903, while on a retreat at the Marist Fathers in Rome in preparation for the Priesthood, I made the acquaintance of a deacon who was attending the Canadian College which is conducted by the Sulpicians, he told me that his Fr. Superior was explaining his book on the priesthood at spiritual reading and that everyone was amazed at it. 'What a great man that Fr. Berthier is! What doctrine! What richness! What persuasiveness! What a great good he is doing for our souls of future priests!"

"*The priest in the preaching ministry*", remarks Bishop Paulot, Vicar General of Reims, "reveals a great acquaintance on the part of the author with pastoral duties and a deep knowledge of St. Alphonsus Liguori, the Doctor of Missionaries. I admit that during my fifteen years as a Missionary I made very good use of this book. All Fr.

Berthier's books, even and especially his *Moral and Dogmatic Theology* are impregnated with his unquestionable dedication to pastoral duties: the sanctification and salvation of souls, the only two things which mean anything to him." **(10)**

"Generally speaking", again remarks Fr. Rivoire, "nothing is ever mentioned about splendor, labored refinements, style, originality and flamboyancy in reference to Fr. Berthier's works; that is true because none of these characteristics are found in his writings. We have often heard people say: 'He has been a great help to me'. Very fine praise indeed. Unstudied, frank and true, praise which is justly deserved, very meaningful and most precise. Fr. Berthier's books do not dazzle the reader – they help him. They are not read out of curiosity or without profit; they are put to good use." **(11)**

One of his great consolations was to see that the seeds which he had sown by the handful in the Field of the Father were productive of unseen but abundant fruit. In all humility, he would often express his happiness and his gratitude to Almighty God, in prospectuses or in footnotes to the pages of his books, for these many great blessings which he had received.

His *The Book for All* which "he would have liked to see in the hands of everybody" was a source of singular satisfaction to him. "God has blessed this book", says he in 1898, "and over 50,000 copies have already been sold." **(12)**

Later on, in 1904, he again mentions this same book: "The many books which I have published for the average person may be read with great profit by all the members of the family; the most useful one however is *The Book for All*, which has been translated into seven languages; we have sold over 100,000 copies of the French edition." **(13)**

Even the books which he had written especially for the clergy were very popular; he, more than anybody else, was surprised at how quickly they were disposed of. He disclosed in one of his advertising notices that 7,000 copies of his *Summary of Dogmatic and Moral theolo-*

gy had been sold in a few months. **(14)** "Our 'Collection of Sermons' is enjoying a circulation beyond anything we could have dared hope for and as of now we have sold over 23,000 copies." **(15)**

During the year of their beloved Founder's death, the Fathers of the Holy Family made the following statement in reference to Fr. Berthier's books which they were publishing: "The French editions of some of our popular books are selling by the hundreds of thousands; we expect to have the same success with our German and Dutch editions." **(16)**

After some close calculating, Fr. Ramers estimated that over a million books of Fr. Berthier had been sold during his lifetime. **(17)**

Fr. Berthier's book, *The Priesthood, its Excellence, Obligations, Rights, Advantages and Privileges*, originally published is 1894

That nineteenth century writer, even among the most famous novelists, could boast of such a large production and lay claim to so great a reputation and popularity? Fr. Berthier did not become proud or self-conceited over his success. Through the numerous editions of his publications he saw only one thing, the good that had to be accomplished and he looked upon his books which were being bought by the thousands as an army of intrepid satellites which he was leading against the combined assaults of an evil and free thinking press.

His one great aim was to do some little good. **(18)** He humbly kept on repeating that "credit for whatever good is accomplished must be given by his readers to the writers from whom he borrows and quotes." **(19)**

Few men have been able, as was Fr. Berthier, to coordinate their works, their writings, their whole life in such a way as to come into contact with all souls, to do good to everyone and reestablish harmony in God. There you have", concludes Fr. Rivoire, "my picture of the Missionary, the writer, the Founder, in one word – the apostle – who lived quite unnoticed at the end of the nineteenth century, a man who made very little noise in the world but did much good." **(20)**

To do good and at the same time to make Our Lady of La Salette known and loved was the double objective of both his special and universal apostolate of the written word. He did more than anyone else, and that by means of his books, to spread the devotion of the Virgin in Tears? His brochures which explain the apparition are spread throughout the world.

The cult of Our Lady of La Salette, we read in the *Annals* of the Holy Mountain in the year 1878, "far from dropping off, seems to be on the increase day by day. We have just received three translations of Fr. Berthier's 'Notice' on the apparition of La Salette. One of these translations comes from Washington, DC, in the United States of America; another comes from Lisbon, Portugal, and we are told that it is selling well; finally the 'Notice' in Italian has a novena included in it and it has been well received by the public. This little book was written for the propose of doing good and it is doing just that." **(21)**

Bishop Cieplak related in America that he had gotten acquainted with the Apparition of La Salette by reading one of Fr. Berthier's books while he was in a Soviet prison in Russia. **(22)** Fr. Berthier always mentioned La Salette when writing and everyone of his books has the recital of the Apparition as well as many practical allusions to her message of September 19, 1846. "Since we are addressing ourselves to children of Mary", he writes in his book, *The Young Lady at the School of the Saints*, "how can we forget to set before them the beautiful example which She, whom we love as a mother, has given them in our own day!" **(23)**

"Blessed are they who pray to Her with confidence", he writes at the end of this book. "Still more blessed are those souls who are docile to her teachings and who mingle their tears with hers, who unite with her in constant prayer and the practice of penance in order to appease the wrath of God. Thrice blessed are they who are not only satisfied to draw spiritual consolations for themselves from her merciful Apparition but also 'make known' to others with whom they come into contact the words of Mary which inspire hatred of sin, especially of blasphemy, of the profanation of the Lord's Day and the violation of the laws of fast and abstinence." **(24)**

His brochures have made known far and wide the story of La Salette and the spirit of penance which it preaches. He has even dedicated one of his masterpieces to *The Marvels of La Salette.*"

Cardinal Benoît-Marie Langénieux, Bishop of Rheims by William Ewart Lockhart

In one of his propaganda pamphlets, he writes as follows: "Failure to work according to one's ability in making known the message of Our Lady of La Salette would clearly indicate a lack of appreciation of the importance this event has in the designs of God. *Well, my children, you will make this known to all my people*; this command was repeated twice to the two shepherds which implies that everyone must be made acquainted not only with the Apparition but also with the teachings which it contains. Christians must, by work and example, instill in others love of interior recollection and self-denial, dispositions which are so necessary to the Christian life.

"There will be great happiness among men when that spirit which our Blessed Mother brought to La Salette is, through the zeal of her children, spread throughout the world to renew the face of the earth."

(25)

Fr. Berthier, more than anyone else, contributed towards hastening that day of happiness by means of his popular writings and the many sermons he preached as a Missionary. **(26)** "It is impossible", he says, "to preach to the people without falling back on the teachings of Our Lady of La Salstte . . . Let us honor her always, especially by being faithful to her teachings." **(27)**

He, more than anyone else, had the happiness and steadfastness to collaborate with the Blessed Virgin in the same program and work of spiritual revival during those days of general indifference. He was the faithful bearer, everywhere, of the teachings of Christ which Mary recalled to our minds on her visit to the Mountain. La Salette and Fr. Berthier are always mentioned in the same breath as we see from the words of the Carthusian monk, Fr. Augustin Rivoire: "When you mention La Salette, you mention Fr. Berthier." **(28)**

Cardinal Benoît-Marie Langénieux (1824-1905) wrote him as follows: "Busy as you are with cares and preoccupations, how are you able to write such lengthy books, so serious and so full of information readily available to the clergy? This is surely a miracle which Our Lady of La Salette is working in you and through you." **(29)**

Endnotes

(1) Propaganda leaflet, p. 7. (1896); (2) Letters to Fr. Douare of Veyssilieu, 2nd letter; (3) Ibidem; (4) Ibidem, 3rd letter; (5) lbidem; (6) De Lombaerde, cited above, p. 331; (7) *The Wonders of La Salette*, p. 337; (8) Excerpts from the first prospectus of 1894; (9) Letter from Fr. Augustin Rivoire, Chartreux and former Missionary of La Salette to Fr. Ramers, Missionary of the Holy Family, March 31, 1927. See Dissertation of Fr. Ramers, Volume, text p. 233; (10) Letter of June 27, 1928 to Fr. Ramers, M.S.F., See Dissertation of Fr. Ramers, Volume, text p. 233; (11) Letter from Fr. Rivoire, ibidem; (12) *The Mother according to the heart of God*, 1898 edition, p. 271. Note 1; (13) The Key of Heaven, 1904 edition, p. 196. Note 1; (14) Prospectus of 1896, p. 15; (15) *The Priest in the Ministry of Preaching or Sermon Collection*, 7th edition, I, p. 7; (16) *The Messenger of the Holy Family*, 1908, p. 616 bis; (17) Letter from Fr. Ramers to the author (1929); (18) *The Priesthood*, Preface p. 10; (19), ibidem; (20) Letter of March 31, 1927 to Fr. Ramers; (21) *Annals of La Salette*, 1878-1879, p. 317; (22) Bulletin of the Works of the Missionaries of La Salette. 1926, p. 142; (23) *The Young Lady and the Christian Virgin at the School of Saints*, (1868), p. 71; (24) *The Young Lady and the Christian Virgin at the School of the Saints*, 10th edition, p. 368; (25) *Our Lady of La Salette, Her Apparition, Her Devotion*, 1892, p. 86; (26) Ibidem; (27) *The Priest in the Ministry of Preaching*, 7th edition, 1st vol., p. 953 and 2nd vol., p.718; (28) Souvenir letter from Fr. Rivoire to Fr. Ramers; (29) Letter written from Reims on January 6, 1896, kept in the archives of the Missionaries of the Holy Family.

9
His Project of "Late Vocations"

Fr. Giraud had collected the main ideas of his doctrine of *Victim and Reparation* from the great Oratorians of the seventeenth century and published them for nineteenth century souls. The best that was in his spirit of sacrifice and life of victim had been borrowed from them.

There is no doubt that it was from their works which he read and reread that Fr. Berthier nourished his great ideal of missionary action which he always kept in mind and placed at the service of the secular clergy. He owes to these same spiritual writers the inspiration he had to take up the work of "late vocations" which occupied him ceaselessly at a time of life when most men think of retiring.

Fr. Charles de Condran (1588-1641)

He wrote in 1894: "Many fortunately have understood what was in the mind of Fr. Charles de Condran (1588-1641) when Fr. Olier wrote the following about him: "Fr. de Condren pointed out to me that it would be the easiest thing in the world to establish and successfully operate a seminary provided we received therein only young men who were a little older than the average beginner; their mature judgment should help them to decide after sufficient probation whether or not they are called to the service of the altar." (1)

Fr. Berthier was won over to this idea of establishing seminaries for young men 'who were a little older than the average beginner', that is, for late vocations'; moreover he was one of the first in France to understand and to put into execution this plan which had been in the mind of the Berullians and the Sulpicians.

He was close to sixty when he undertook the splendid task of founding the Institute of the Holy Family, not without some trepidation at his own audacity.

"Do you think that I am too old", he asked Cardinal Mariano Rampolla del Tindaro (1843-1913) at an important audience, held in November 1894, "to undertake a work of this nature?" "You are anything but too old", smilingly replied the prelate. "God has inspired this project. He will give you the years and the strength to bring it to a successful conclusion; go ahead with your work." (2)

He had personally been a precocious vocation and had the experience of a lifetime practically wholly dedicated to the training of young men for the priesthood. Now, late in life, with renewed zeal and youth, he was taking up the work of late vocations and was preparing to initiate an intensive campaign to promote an enterprise which had been on his mind for quite some time and which would eventually prove to be so helpful in the care of souls.

"It very often happens", he states in his work on *The Priesthood*, "that young men who have led very good lives amid the dangers of the world give better guarantees of leading a holy life later on than do many young boys, who, because they have been kept away from the allurements of sin, are not disciplined for the struggle. When Our Lord chose his Apostles, they were no longer children. We are quite familiar with the fact that Saint Ignatius and Saint Camillus de Lellis began learning grammar when they were thirty years old. The latter was often a target for the mockery of his younger fellow students who used to say to him: *Tarde venisti* (*you have come late*). Their teacher used to silence them by predicting that he would do far much more good than the others even though he did start late. Let us take care not to neglect our 'late vocations'" (3)

In the many propaganda notices which he sent everywhere, he made it a point to list the names of great saints who entered the priesthood late in life as well as those of illustrious bishops such as Bishop

Emmanuel Frieherr von Ketteler (1811-1877) of Mayence and Cardinal Paul Melchers (1813-1895), Archbishop of Cologne, both of whom were bright luminaries of the Church towards the end of the last (nineteenth) century after living a long time in the world." (4)

He loved to recount the story of Adolph Kolping (1813-1965) who "became very famous in Germany. He was a shoemaker before studying for the priesthood; after his ordination he founded the great society known as 'The Catholic Workers' which is very widespread in Germany, Austria, Switzerland, Holland and many other places . . ." (5)

Then too- there is the story of "Jimmy" who used to tie labels on wheat sacks, later on known as Cardinal James Gibbons (1834-1921). "How could we forget Fr. Gerin, one of the priests delegated by Bishop de Bruillard, ordinary of Grenoble, to take the secrets of La Salette to Pope Pius IX? He also was a shoemaker; he made his studies for the priesthood as best he could, was finally ordained and later on in life was greatly admired because of his great priestly zeal; he was an excellent orator and his sermons were very effective in moving the hearts of his auditors (listeners). The bishop appointed him Pastor of the Cathedral of Grenoble and Vicar General of the Diocese; he died in the odor of sanctity during his tenure of these offices." (6)

Cardinal Mariano Rampolla del Tindaro

Fr. Berthier had at his disposal countless stories and innumerable arguments to explain his project and, if need be, to defend it against inconceivable scorn and criticism. His great ambition was to supply the Church not necessarily with saints and illustrious personages but with good workers coming at a late hour to labor in the vineyard of the Master.

"Seven-eighths of the world's population of this Twentieth Century are still in the darkness of infidelity, heresy or schism, he stated in 1902; "Three quarters of humanity do not know Our Blessed Lord; businessmen and tradesmen are exploiting the land of the infidel in large numbers whereas the laborers in the mission field preaching the gospel to the aborigines are far too few." **(7)**

He was not long in relieving the shortage of missionaries through his work of "late vocations", one similar to that undertaken by Fr. Feron in France and in England. In 1894, in a footnote of his book, *Le Sacerdote (The Priesthood)*, where he gives the addresses of several residences of Fr. Feron, he states the following: "With the blessing of His Holiness Leo XIII we are undertaking a project similar to Fr. Feron's for the foreign missions. If God blesses this work, we will gladly receive young men not subject to military service who are recommended to us by our confreres because of their virtue, their intelligence, their zeal and their attraction to the apostolate." **(8)**

Fr. Berthier had contemplated for a long time the possibility of taking up a project of this nature, one that would foster the vocations of young men, more or less advanced in age, who felt called to the priesthood and missionary life. While he was director of the Apostolic School at Saint-Joseph and also when he was in charge of the Scholasticate at La Souste, he felt that something should be done to take care of late vocations and he would have liked even then to put into execution the ideas which were constantly haunting him.

The age limit which was fourteen had obliged him to turn down the applications of many young men for admissions; this regulation of the Apostolic School was strictly adhered to. In his first brochure, *The Work of Vocations to La Salette*, he confides that over forty applications a year were received for admission to the school and this number would no doubt have doubled, were it not generally known that students over fourteen years of age were not usually accepted." **(9)**

He had made more than one exception to this regulation which limited the age of admission to fourteen. He wrote as follows later on to defend himself against possible criticism: "Let us not forget that the Catholic Missions everywhere are in need of laborers; even today in France it is difficult to obtain missionaries to preach missions in our parishes; the parochial clergy is steadily decreasing in number and this fact, according to serious minds, is one of the greatest dangers to the Church in France during this twentieth century."

"How can we help to ward off this danger? By building Apostolic Schools, more and more of them. These schools which train missionaries are like the roots of the great tree to which the spread of the gospel is compared; if the roots are lacking, how will this tree spread its branches and cover the earth with its protective shade? . . . It has been difficult because of military laws or other reasons to receive in these schools young men who are older than the average beginner." (10)

From that time on, he took the steps necessary to found a school for 14 to 30-year-old young men, exempt from military service and able to pursue the required course of studies, men who would be given the opportunity of later on joining the ranks of the priestly or missionary army and thus increase its numbers and its strength.

The Call of the Church, of Christ and of the Blessed Virgin

It was the powerful voice of Leo XIII that roused him to action. He had listened to the "sorrowful complaints" and "the pathetic exhortations of His Holiness in his Encyclical of December 3, 1880, in which he stated "that the number of saintly workers is diminishing day by day." (11) This same voice was even more pleading through "its expressions of sorrow in a later Encyclical, addressed to the Princes and the Nation, June 26, 1894, after the festivities commemorating his episcopal jubilee (an encyclical which could be called the swan song and last testament of this great pontiff)." (12)

"We daily beseech the divine goodness", he said among other things, "to multiply the number of sacred ministers who will fulfill perfectly the duties of their apostolic calling; that is, men dedicated to the spreading of the kingdom of Christ even at the cost of their personal comfort, their health and their very life if necessary." (13)

Brazilian version of Our Lady of La Salette

The voice of Our Lady of La Salette was also urging him to spread still further and with greater speed the Marian message which was a reminder of the gospel teaching of her Divine Son to whom mankind was unwilling to submit.

"Vocation work", he stated with the deepest conviction, "is the work of the Sacred Heart of Jesus who desires to make others sharers of his love through the ministry of those who work out of love of him; it is also the work of the Heart of Mary who wants apostles for the purpose of making her message and her tears known to all her people. It is essentially the work of all those who love Our Lord and his divine Mother." (14)

He will now take up his new work with a firm determination because his love of the church, his dedication to Christ and the Blessed Virgin impelled him to take up this project which was par excellence the work of the hearts of Jesus and Mary. The idea of establishing an Apostolic School for "late vocations" for the missions was most dear to him and he would start on this project as soon as possible under the guiding hand of Providence.

Priests' Retreats at Reims

In 1888, he was back again at his old work of preaching retreats and missions, ministry which he had set aside for years in order to devote himself to the training of young men for the priesthood. He was constantly on the go until 1894, giving his best to this apostolic work which he loved so much. One of his trips brought him to Reims where he had been called by the Archbishop, Cardinal Benoît Langénieux (1824-1905), to preach the diocesan retreat to his priests.

He received a fine welcome from the Cardinal and made use of this opportunity to speak to him about his most cherished project. the prelate was satisfied to listen to the missionary, advised him to do nothing precipitously, to pray and allow the project to mature." **(15)**

The Cardinal had been so impressed by the zeal of the preacher that he invited him again to preach the following year; he attended all the exercises of the retreat and had many conversations with Fr. Berthier. This time however he was all enthusiasm for the project and promised to give Fr. Berthier all possible assistance; he was going to Rome in a few months and he would speak to the Holy Father about it.

The Founder of the Missionaries of the Holy Family afterwards wrote in reference to this: "Before putting this project into execution, it had to be first of all submitted to him who takes the place of God here on earth, whose approval of a work is a guarantee of God's blessing upon it." **(16)**

This decision of the eminent Cardinal to come, as it were, to the rescue of the zealous and enterprising missionary, gave a new impetus to the enthusiasm he had been holding back for some, time now? An appointment was made for a meeting in home and they got together there on November 12, 1894.

In Rome

St. Peter's Square and Basilica in 1909

Cardinal Langenieux later on attested "that he introduced Fr. Berthier to His Eminence Cardinal Rampella so that this project which he had judged to be so promotive of the glory of God could be fully explained to him; the Cardinal Secretary asked him at their meeting to write a complete outline of the proposed work for the Holy Father, promising that he would deliver it in person to His Holiness on the following day, November 13, 1894." (17)

The Secretary of State was most enthusiastic over the proposed foundation and saw "in it an inspiration of God to take care of problems of great concern with which he was well acquainted." (18)

Fr. Berthier immediately wrote down for the Holy Father "the advantages of an Institute whose purpose was to receive from every nation young men who desired to become missionaries and who up to now had been unable to make the required course of studies. They would be prepared fore the apostolic life, first by an abbreviated course depending on the age and needs of the individual, then by a regular novitiate and profession of the three simple vows and finally by a course in Philosophy and Theology. The Institute would, of course, be autonomous as its important enough purpose would demand. The members would first of all establish residences in different countries for the purpose of admitting young men of a certain age who felt called to the apostolate. Finally, once they became sufficiently numerous, they would offer themselves to the Sacred Congregation of the Propaganda to be sent to the foreign missions." (19)

Cardinal Langenieux was received in a private audience by the Pope on November 14 and made the following remarks after it: "Imagine my surprise on learning that the Holy Father was fully informed on this project and determined to give all possible support. "It is a most opportune world", His Holiness said to me, "and it is my wish that it be started as soon as possible." He then requested me to become its Protector and give Fr. Berthier all possible assistance in establishing this foundation. Whatever objections I brought up were easily dispelled and the Vicar of Christ gave me whatever powers I would need to enable Fr. Berthier to initiate this new work towards which his zeal and the manifest designs of Providence ware directing him." **(20)**

Approbation of His Project

There was to be no more hesitating; Providence was now leading him along the path he was to travel for the rest of his life.

'The first thing we did after receiving the encouragement and blessing of the Holy Father was to draw up the regulations of this "Foundation"; next we submitted them to His Eminence Cardinal Langenieux at the beginning of January 1895; he approved these and the project itself in two separate decisions". **(21)**

The next step was to establish a residence somewhere in France or in some foreign land. "Foreseeing", he said, "that France would soon banish Religious Institutes, or at the very least would impose stricter controls on their freedom of action, we thought of beginning our work in a more liberal country"; from Reims he went to Holland, "a land so hospitable and peaceful." **(22)**

The Foundation in Holland

At La Salette he had made the acquaintance of Pilgrims from Tilbourg and on his arrival in Holland, at the end of January 1895, he went directly to them, to obtain whatever information he needed. "These devoted friends", as he called them, led him to the Pastor of the Cathedral of Bois-le-Duc and he in turn introduced him to Bishop Wilhelm Van de Ven.

His Grace received him well and said to him: "Look for a suitable place in my diocese and I will approve whatever you choose." **(23)**

"This was in mid-Winter", writes the pioneer, "Northern Brabant was at that time covered with snow and it was not easy to get a correct estimate of locations suitable for the foundation of our project. We entrusted to our Dutch friends the task of looking around for a place that would suit our needs, for rent or for sale, and we left the Brabant to return again in the middle of March.

"Saint Joseph, to whom we had entrusted our enterprise, came to our assistance in a most wonderful way. After much looking around, we had found only one moderately priced place; in Grave, a city mentioned by Bossuet in his "History of the World." We providentially came upon a large barracks and a military hospital which had been evacuated three years previously and was now the property of the city. Mr. Friesen, Burgomaster of Grave and presently a deputy in the Lower Chamber of Holland, graciously offered to sell us, at a very reasonable price, the two houses, the garden which adjoins the hospital and the large field next to the barracks where the soldiers used to drill; the entire property had an area of over one hectare and was surrounded by a wall which once protected Grave when it was a fortified city."

Wilhelm Van de Ven (1834-1919), Bishop of Bois-le-Duc, Netherlands

"Everything was far from being in the best of condition; we placed our project, with the approbation of Carinal Langerieux, under the protection of The Holy Family which had never lived in palaces in Bethlehem, in Egypt or at Nazareth; since our purpose was to train Missionaries imbued with a missionary spirit, men who would know how to get along with very little and be able to suffer privations for the honor of God and the good of souls, since, in the second place, the location was naturally beautiful, there being many elm trees about the property, some of which shade the front of the barracks, and finally, since there was plenty of room for future expansion, we purchased the property at the end of March 1895, after consulting Bishop Wilhelm Van de Ven of Bois-le-Duc. (Burgomeister Friesen was with us on that occasion). We moved in at the end of September of the same year." **(24)**

What a long sentence, balanced like a tight battalion, ready to conquer the world, or more humbly taking possession of an old barracks from where was going to leave a new army of apostles, equipped to the old and rough way!

The Installation

"As soon as we were installed", continues the same narrator, "the Bishop gave us the necessary approbation as he had promised; he also allowed us to follow the rules which had been approved by Cardinal Langenieux. He delegated the local pastor, Fr. John Sprangers, to bless the two houses and the two chapels, one of which was in the barracks, the other in the former hospital; from then on the Holy Sacrifice was offered in what used to be the living quarters of Dutch soldiers. **(25)**

Mr. Friesen, Bourgomeister of Grave, Netherlands, warmly welcomes Fr. Berthier to his city

These beginnings were similar to those of La Souste; they were difficult days. Fr. Berthier had become accustomed and inured to the trials of pioneers from his early days at Saint-Joseph. Here is what he says: "The early years were painfully employed in training a nucleus of virtuous, devoted, pious and well-intentioned young men who would be models of regularity for those who were to come after them." **(26)**

They came from everywhere and from all ranks of life after he had inserted an announcement of his foundation in the principal Catholic papers of France and Germany. His chief concern was to select the right candidates from among the many applications; "During the first years up to 1902", he writes, "we have had each year an average of one hundred applications for admission." **(27)**

He was far from fortunate in his choice of candidates; that was due to the fact that there was such a mixture of everything among the new arrivals. We can repeat in the humble words of Fr. Berthier that "the first years were the least happy ones." **(28)** The first biographer of the Founder does not hesitate to say that "the number of defections was appalling and on more than one occasion, there was reason to believe that the whole project would be shipwrecked." **(29)** He read the following in Fr. Patarin's notes; "Many of these defections were no doubt due to some of the helpers Fr. Berthier had about himself in the early days of the enterprise; some of them relished very little the spirit of poverty and sacrifice which the Founder was trying to develop in his young men."

Fr. Berthier took very good care of his little "ship"; he refitted it when needed, made the necessary repairs; his unshakeable confidence kept it afloat is spite of winds and storms. Calm and harmony was gradually restored among those young men who had embarked at a rather late hour to sail among the reefs and obstacles of the religious life and the priesthood.

It took no less than ten years of continued effort, obstinate perseverance and endless work to pilot them to port. Only three of these hundreds of early applicants ultimately reached the priesthood but these had been well trained and served as wonderful examples to the many valiant priests who later on followed in their footsteps.

During this long and painful period which began with the foundation in 1895 and ended with the first Ordinations to the Priesthood in 1905, he became again what he had formerly been in Switzerland, professor of rhetoric, of philosophy and theology, a handicraftsman at manual labor, an intellectual worker in the composition of new books while at the same time supervising the management of the former Dutch barracks.

Success of His Project

The day he announced his first ordinations to the priesthood was his great day of triumph, and glory.

"Our readers and the charitable souls who are interested in the work of the Holy Family", he wrote in his victory bulletin dated September, 1905 "will learn with great pleasure that three of our young men had the happiness of being ordained priests August 20, the Feast of St. Joachim, and they celebrated their First Masses on the 21st. That was an occasion of celebration and great rejoicing in the community of The Holy Family. The Reverend Dean and pastor of Grave who has been most helpful, benevolent in our regard from the beginning of our enterprise, most graciously assisted one of our new priests at the altar. The Burgomeister of Grave ,who welcomed us with open arms to his city and who is always ready to be of service to us, was a guest at the festivities as was also the curate of Grave." (30)

He no longer thought of his former hardships; neither was he mindful of himself, preferring to give the places of honor to his friends

Church bell for the Basilica tower on the Holy Mountain
arrives by mule train on July 17, 1897

and benefactors. During the next three years, the last of his life, he was to gradually retire to the background, handing over the reins of government to the younger hands of his eldest sons. They will number at the time of his death in 1908, 25 priests, 13 deacons, 10 clerics in minor orders and 160 **(31)** students. In 1929 there were 190 priests, 188 scholastics and student novices and 121 lay brothers, professed and novices. **(32)**

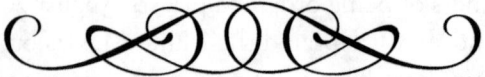

Endnotes

(1) *The Priesthood*, 1894 edition, p. 32; (2) De Lombaerde, cited above, p.387; (3) *The Priesthood*, p. 32; (4) *The Work of the Holy Family for Belated Apostolic Vocations*, Grave 1902, p. 8; (5) Ibidem; (6) Ibidem, p. 9; See the portrait of Fr. Gerin in our book on *The Cures at La Salette*; (7) *The Work of the Holy Family*, p. 3; (8) The Priesthood, p. 32, note 1; (9) *The Work of Vocations at La Salette*, 1884 edition, p. 128; (10) The Work of the Holy Family, p. 9; (11) *The Vocation Work at La Salette*, 1887 edition, p.14. - *The Work of the Holy Family*, p. 3; (12) *The Work of the Holy Family*, p. 4; (13) Encyclical of June 26, 1894 quoted in *the Work of the Holy Family*, p. 5; (14) *The Work of Vocations at La Salette*, 1884 edition, p. 129; (15) De Lombaerde, cited above, p. 380-394. Chap. 8: The big project. Fr. Ramers speaks only of a retreat at Reims, from August 20-24, 1894; (16) *The Work of the Holy Family*, p. 12; (17) Certificate of Dec. 25 1905 preserved in the Archives of the Institute of the Holy Family and graciously communicated by Fr. Ramers; (18) Letter of November 25,1894 written by Cardinal Langenieux to Very Reverend Fr. Auguste Chapuy (1826-1907), Superior General of the Missionaries of La Salette; (19) Certificate of Cardinal Langenieux. Ibidem; (20) Cardinal Langenieux's letter to Very Reverend Fr. Chapuy. – De Lombaerde, cited above, p. 388; (21) *The Work of the Holy Family*, p. 12; (22) *The Work of the Holy Family*, p. 13; (23) Ibidem and De Lombaerde,

cited above, p. 397; (24) *The Work of the Holy Family*, p. 14. – From De Lombaerde, cited above, p. 397 and following; (25) Ibidem; (26) *The Work of the Holy Family*, p. 15; (27) Ibidem; (28) Ibidem; (29) De Lombaerde, cited above, p. 432. See some statistics on this subject, in particular p. 433, 454, 455, 464, 466, 468, 564. – "A lot of defections were probably due to the auxiliaries that Fr. Berthier had assistant to his initial work and were far to taste the spirit of poverty and sacrifice he tried to instill in his dear young people. *Notes of Fr. Patarin*; (30) De Lombaerde, cited above, p. 475; (31) Ibidem, p. 570; (32) Summary statistics in *Schematismus* (*Yearbook*), M.S.F. for 1929, that is, from the *Ordo*.

10

His New Foundation
— A Sequel to La Salette —

Fr. Berthier wrote as follows at the end of his hook, *Les Merveilles de La Salette*: "Allow me to say a word about a work which falls in with the wishes of Our Lady of La Salette; it is the work of 'late vocations for the missions'." (1)

Fr. Jean Berthier, M.S.

He goes on to explain in the last pages of this book the importance and the usefulness of the work he had just undertaken with the blessing of Pope Leo XIII and the approbation of Cardinal Langenieux.

"May this project", he adds, with confidence and quasi-prophetic assurances, "aided by the prayers of fervent souls, play its part in the fulfillment of everything which the message of La Salette implies and may it contribute its share in making known to all her people the teachings of this divine Mother and the significance of her tears." (2)

Let us add in conclusion that he was perfectly correct in speaking so and characterizing his project as one of the "wonderful things" born of the Apparition of La Salette; his work is an extraordinary marvel of success and beauty thanks to the hidden, yet evident cooperation of her who inspired him to undertake it.

He categorically states in one of his brochures, *The Work of The Holy Family for late vocations to the apostolate*, that this idea of his and its execution were both inspired by the Apparition of La Salette.

He writes as follows: "It was in answer to the recommendation of Our Lady of La Salette: *Well, my children, you will make this known to all my people*, twice made to the witnesses of the Apparition, that I conceived the idea of taking up this work, the special aim of which was to receive intelligent and pious young merit, regardless of nationality, who felt called to the missions yet could not gain admission to other educational institutions because of their age or the lack of available financial means." (3)

Universality is the hallmark of La Salette; it is also the stamp that marks Fr. Berthier's work. He will often repeat, as he states in the Rules of the Community of the Holy Family which hand down to us this personal testimony of his, "that he first conceived his project on the Mountain of La Salette." (4)

Fr. Berthier's purpose in initiating this last undertaking, the most astounding and audacious one of his active career, was to further fulfill the mandate of the Virgin of La Salette. He never entertained the thought of breaking away from a past that had given birth to his future work and which would be a guarantee of its success. He intended to remain a Missionary of La Salette while he followed the new course outlined for him by Providence.

His New Work in Keeping with His Salettine Vocation

Some there were who mistakenly feared he might deviate in a greater or lesser degree from the spirit of his Salettine vocation. This apprehension could exist only in the minds of those who had a very poor knowledge of Fr. Berthier. He never could have entertained the least thought of renouncing or turning away from the ideal of his life, the soul of his soul, his firm and tireless devotedness to the service of Our Lady of La Salette. The fact is that the Weeping Virgin wanted him as a more intimate partner in the apostolate and entrusted him with a most difficult undertaking, one which he would bring to a successful issue by dint of perseverance and superabundant energy.

He answered a letter of one of his penitents who was very much alarmed at the thought that he would cease being a Missionary of La Salette; she later on remarked that she had "never seen anything so beautiful and so humble." Expressing regret at having destroyed the letter, she gave the following resume of its contents: "My child, I will never leave the community. Certainly I am not indispensable; others will do just as good work as I did and even better. However, when I see so many young men, older than the average beginner, who want to study for the priesthood, when I think of all those 'late vocations' I feel called to establish a new work. Later on perhaps, conditions in France being what they are, there may be a shortage of priests; my project will help to supply men to fill in the need. I am leaving home but my heart will always be there." (5)

One of his spiritual sons later on reechoed these same sentiments of Fr. Berthier whose life was a continual act of love for his September 19, 1846 Virgin.

"He used to often say that the Institute of the Holy Family was born on the mountain of La Salette, under the very eyes and in the tears of the Blessed Virgin. When Mary selected this young deacon to be the herald of her voice and the mouthpiece of her complaints, she also wanted him to be the founder of a new congregation which, though not bearing her name, would dedicate itself to the cult of her tears and her sorrows.

"It was at La Salette that the Virgin inspired the pious missionary with this bold idea, so productive of results; it was at La Salette too that he who made this idea a reality meditated on it and nurtured it by means of his prayers and supplications. It was from there also that he departed to begin his work in a distant land, far from Mary's Mountain yet close to the heart of his heavenly Messenger.

"Does not this show and prove that this is a work of the Mother of God, an offshoot of her glorious Apparition, one of the tears of Our

Lady of la Salette?

The tears of Mary are tears of the heart and each tear is a seed of love, of devotion, of sacrifice." **(6)**

He was somewhat disturbed by this inspiration, which was calling him away and he reflected a long time before coming to a decision; once he was sure of the call, nothing stopped him. He calmly took all the necessary steps to go where the spirit of God called him, all the while remaining a Missionary of La Salette, his heart, his filled at the cost of deep and tormenting anxieties.

His Relations with the Institute of the Missionaries

We can well imagine the embarrassment of a worker called to labor in a distant field, of an Assistant General of one community who contemplated founding another, independent of his own and autonomous. Would he be accused of desertion or at least of ingratitude if not of ambition?

Many steps were taken, many meetings held, not to put the project into execution but just to clear the way for it according to rules and regulations. Cardinal Langenieux who was his adviser did everything possible to remove many difficulties which at first seemed insurmountable.

The illustrious Archbishop of Reims became at once the intermediary between Fr. Berthier and his superiors. On November 25, 1894, he wrote to Fr. Auguste Chapuy (1826-1907), who had succeeded Fr. Archier as Superior General and among other things said: "It is indeed true that the Holy Father has approved, praised, encouraged and blessed Fr. Berthier's project for 'late vocations'." After mentioning the meetings he had had with Cardinal Rampolla and Leo XIII, he goes on to say: "You may without the least fear give full encouragement to this enterprise in which your Congregation will find an occasion to be of service to the Church; the only sacrifice you are asked to make is to allow one of its members to follow freely a calling which comes from God since the Holy See has judged it to be so." (7)

The Cardinal wrote to Fr. Berthier the same day in order to reassure him and relieve him of many worries: "I have just received a letter from your superior requesting me to inform him on what happened in Rome. I told him everything and asked him to give his full cooperation to a project which had been so highly recommended by the Holy Father. I also informed him that I had been given charge of it and had received all the necessary powers. Be at peace now and thank God who has been so good to you. Please pray for your Cardinal Protector and father." (8)

The La Salette Residence in Rome on Via Cavour

Fr. Berthier, who wanted to offend no one, thanked him in a letter written from Joseph-Chanrion Street the following December 4th. It follows here: "I have received your Eminence's letter written to me from Paris. It was a source of great consolation to me. The Rev. Fr. General received the letter you directed to him and he communicated its contents to me immediately. The good father understood that the Holy Father authorized me to take up this work and made no remarks to me on that score. I had told him previously that, since the elections had not yet taken place, I was not available for any position of authority because I wanted to be more free to pursue my work. He was not of the same opinion as I, saying that I could busy myself with this project and still remain in some charge. So I was reelected Assistant with the option of handing in my resignation if circumstances made it necessary to do so. The good father was more considerate than ever in my regard; he has given me permission to recruit subjects and I am thinking of doing just that." **(9)**

The cardinal had received certain powers from Rome and Fr. Berthier, in keeping with his vow of poverty, applied to him for permission "to make certain useful and necessary expenses", especially "to set aside one-half of the revenue accruing from the sale of his books for the purpose of carrying on his work, leaving the other half to his community." **(10)**

The Cardinal lost no time in sending him the necessary permissions and authorization in a short note, written from Reims on December 6; later on, December 20, he wrote a longer letter to set him at ease, encourage him and dispel some of his anxieties.

> "You can honestly say that you not only have been authorized to take up this work of 'late vocations' but that you have been commanded to do so by the Holy Father because he judged this work most useful and opportune ...
>
> "You may add that in order to make the work of this undertaking all the easier and to show his interest in this matter, His Holiness has given me all the faculties and powers necessary to carry on this project; this was done so that you might be perfectly free to act and have no qualms of conscience as regards your vows and the obligations you owe your community ...
>
> "All these questions must be discussed amicably with your superiors but on the basis of the facts which I have just set before you. Let them assist you as much as they can; they will thus acquiesce to the wishes of the Holy Father and they will some day, through your endeavors, receive precious help in

their own work and partake of the many blessings which are assured you ...

"To my mind, it would be a sad thing indeed if you had to separate yourself from your community to carry on your work properly. I am sure that your religious family would not want that to happen; I feel sure that your superiors will allow you full freedom to pursue your work according to the instructions of the Holy Father which I have made known to your venerable Superior General." (11)

He had never dreamed of separating himself from his community; he brought everything into play, especially his humility, to make sure that no such thing would happen; it was a possibility however and the thought had even come to the mind of his Protector. He was greatly comforted when on January 11, 1895, he received an official document from the General Council which stated, "that at the request of Fr. Jean Berthier, Missionary of La Salette, the General Council authorizes him to occupy himself with the work of 'late vocations for the foreign missions', a project requested and encouraged by the Sovereign Pontiff and his Eminence Cardinal Langenieux." (12)

His bond of love and strong attachment to his community of La Salette would remain unbroken. The Cardinal did what he could to strengthen these bonds all the more by means of a letter which he wrote January 22, 1895, to the Superior General of the La Salette Missionaries.

"I understand your preoccupations", he wrote, "concerning the project of good Fr. Berthier. It rests more with you than it does with him to eliminate these by accepting as a blessing for your religious family what you now look upon as a serious danger.

"Now that your Council has authorized him to take up a work which Leo XIII has encouraged and blessed, one over which he has appointed me Protector and auxiliary, there is nothing left to do but to strengthen the bonds which bind this excellent religious indissolubly to a society of which he is a member and which will benefit from the labors of this man of God.

"My Venerable and dear Father, do not be alarmed by the little difficulties of a separation which will be apparent only, and look forward with joy and confidence to this new life which lies ahead of you. Tell everyone and publish it everywhere, that you are proud to see one of your sons, who is united to you in spirit and physically in your midst during the pilgrimage season, entrusted with such a great work, one which will supply the Church as well as your own religious family with Missionaries, one which will recover for the service of God sincere vocations which would otherwise be lost were it not for this new work." (13)

Fr. Berthier was and would remain a Missionary of La Salette; in that capacity, he founded the Institute of the Holy Family. In his first circular after the General Chapter of 1897, the new Superior General, Fr. Perrin, who had succeeded Fr. Chapuys, announced that Fr. Berthier, a fellow novice of his, would rank in precedence after the Assistants General and would, as was the case with Fr. Archier, have a consultative voice in the sessions of the General Council." (14)

Fr. Jean Berthier and Fr. Joseph Perrin

Fr. Perrin in one of his circulars which he addressed to the whole community on August 5, 1907, spoke very highly of Fr. Berthier and referred to him as a masterful recruiter. "Fr. Berthier has by himself been able to bring together as many as 150 subjects to his Holy Family residence in Grave, Holland and he has already led fifteen of these to the priesthood." (15)

Fr. Berthier in turn was always interested in the accomplishments of Fr. Perrin; he was deeply affected on learning that he had been exiled from La Salette and had been compelled to seek asylum in a foreign land.

"I have received no word from Fr. Perrin in a long time", he wrote to Fr. Beaup, the Master of Novices. A letter from France informs me that he was very much affected by all this. Console him as much as you can in your letters. To be banished at his age from everything to which he had dedicated a whole lifetime of work is difficult enough; the fact that he has never lived in a foreign land makes his exile that much more trying. As for us, we have become accustomed to this and being away is rather easy enough."

Fr. Berthier took up with courage, great peace of soul, and with a conscience greatly at ease this new work to which the hand of Providence had guided him.

Immediately on his installation at Grave, "he had one of his students who was a statuary-maker make a statue of Our Lady of La Salette and the Apostolics made it a practice to gather about it to honor Mary and to perform their religious exercises." **(16)**

Fr. Berthier is Helped in His Work by the Missionaries of La Salette

from left: Frs. Fernand Patarin (1862-1939) and Frederick Pons (1827-1905)

His superiors always remained on most amicable terms with him and gave him the loan of two excellent Missionaries to assist him in founding his school; these were, first Fr. Fernand Patarin (1862-1939) and later on Fr. Frédérick Pons (1827-1905). Everyone who saw these two missionaries at work asserts that they were of invaluable assistance and were, each in turn, the right hand man of the Founder.

Fr. Patarin joined Fr. Berthier during a crisis that could have had very serious consequences; during his entire stay which extended from the end of July, 1898, to the beginning of April, 1901, he did his best to ward off the danger, arriving just in tine to give the "nucleus of students the benefit of his devotedness and experience."

Fr. Patarin was himself a late vocation. Fr. Berthier had admitted him to the Apostolic School and directed him on to the priesthood; he was therefore equal to the task at hand. During his stay there of a little more than two years, the number of defections fell off noticeably and the little community "began to feel that it was resting on rather solid ground." **(17)**

We have the following from the notes of Fr. Patarin: "When I associated myself with the Holy Family Project, the students were not very numerous, possibly ten a dozen at the most, four of these eventually reached the priesthood, among then the immediate successor of Fr. Berthier as Superior General. I was his helper from August, 1896, to the first days of April, 1901, about two years and eight months. Fr. Pons arrived at Grave a short time before my departure. On my recall to France I was assigned to the residence of Grenoble, on Joseph-Chanrion Street, to prepare for the preaching ministry. At the time of our exodus in October, 1901, I went with the students of our Apostolic School to Tournai where I worked in the capacity of Prefect until 1905."

Fr. Patarin was recalled to France and accompanied the student body of the Apostolic School to Belgium when it went into exile; he was immediately replaced by Fr. Pons who continued to give the same good service and fine example. The following flattering eulogy is given of him: "Since his arrival here in 1901, the number of students has doubled; rich and numerous blessings have come down to us from heaven and have fostered in everyone a great love of prayer, a thirst for souls as well as a great spirit of sacrifice."

Fr. Pons died on the very day that the three first priests of the Institute of the Holy Family celebrated their First Masses; Fr. Berthier, mingling tears of sorrow with those of joy, made the following announcement at the end of the family feast: "To crown the events of this happy day, Fr. Pons went to God while Mass was being celebrated." **(18)**

Grave house chapel

Fr. Berthier, writing in his Messenger of the Holy Family, gives us the following: "This was a day of prayer and pious songs; there were tears also for it was the day on which our good Father Frédérick Pons died. He had been a Missionary of La Salette for over forty years and my helper since April, 1901; he contributed very much to the formation of our young men by means of his piety and great zeal; he was ill only three weeks and gave his soul back to God at the end of the First Masses celebrated by our first newly-ordained priests. His death was peaceful, as was his life. I am sure that Our Lady of La Salette was in his case the Gate of Heaven." (19)

Thus it was that through the fraternal and comforting cooperation of his own Institute, Fr. Berthier was able to establish his own enterprise of "late vocations" on a solid basis and fully equip it to carry on the good fight of the Lord.

His Love of Our Lady of La Salette

He loved to return to the Holy Mountain during the pilgrimage season to renew his spiritual strength at the feet of Her who had been such a source of comfort to him in his many trials. On his return to Grave, he would kindle the hearts of his dear young men with the flames of his great love of Mary. Fr. Patarin relates that "'every now and then he would speak to his children about the teachings of Mary on the Holy Mountain and the Weeping Mother was as much invoked in his residence as she was in any house of our own community. In our heart to heart talks", continues the same Missionary of La Salette, "the Rev. Father enjoyed discussing our works and often spoke about the different members of the Congregation; although his heart was divided since he became the Father of a new family, his love of the first never diminished." (20)

"My children", he used to say to his young men, "have a great devotion to Our Lady of La Salette for it is to her that we owe everything we are today; pay her great honor; I insist on that very much because I have dedicated my priestly life for Her. I owe her all the credit for the little bit of good I have been able to accomplish; without her help, we would not be here, neither you nor I; consequently you owe her not only your vocation but also all the good you will one day be able to accomplish.

"I enjoy seeing you kiss the feet of her statue and dedicate yourselves to Her; continue this custom; by so doing you help me to pay a debt of gratitude which I owe Her. Later on this devotion must be handed down to every residence of our Congregation; it

Grave classroom where Fr. Berthier worked among his students; notice the bust of Fr. Berthier in the background

will be an efficient means of nurturing the spirit of mortification, obedience and poverty which the Virgin preaches by word and by deed." (21)

The first offshoot of his Institute was named after Our Lady of La Salette. As the barrack-convent- had become too small to accommodate the numerous personnel, he bought a neighboring dye shop and transformed it into an Apostolic School. He chose September 19, 1903, anniversary of the Apparition, as opening day of the new residence; the statue of the Virgin in tears was carried in solemn procession there on that occasion.

"At two o'clock in the afternoon, the entire community assembled in the garden of the new residence. The statue of the most Blessed Virgin, carried by four Apostolics, was welcomed at the entrance of the property and accompanied in solemn procession to the chapel as 140 voices sang with love and devotion:

> "O, Our Lady of La Salette
> We come to weep with Thee;
> The storm is close at hand,
> Pray for the Church and us."

Fr. Sprangers, the venerable Dean of Grave, had come to enhance the ceremony by his presence; he blessed the chapel and afterwards the statue of the Blessed Virgin. After a few warm and edifying words, the good Dean gave Benediction at the request of Fr. Berthier; this was followed by general rejoicing. The Virgin of La Salette now numbered among her shrines a little sanctuary in Holland, her devoted servant, faithful to his promise, had again made known Mary's word "to all her people." **(22)**

His Death

Fr. Berthier's memorial card

A few months before he died, he had felt the need of retiring somewhere in solitude so as to better prepare himself for death. He spent six days with the Cistercians of Corpus Christi, at Nieuwkuijk, Holland. While there he reviewed his whole life, going back year by year to the days before his religions life and priesthood. He went back in memory to the conversations he formerly had had with Fr. Archier who had been his spiritual director. "In this manner our good Father Berthier was able to commune in spirit with his former director whom he always held in the highest esteem and whom he venerated as a saint." **(23)**

As a Missionary of La Salette, he always wore the crucifix. When he walked alone, he usually held it in his hands or pressed it tenderly to his heart. To anyone who was familiar with his habits of prayer or knew how careful he was to conceal his acts of love from others, it was evident that his handling of the crucifix was a sign that he was elevating his mind to God and meditating on the sorrows of his Master and those of the Virgin of La Salette." (24)

He died on the 16th of October, 1908, 9 and was buried three days later on the 19th the day of the month which recalls the Apparition of La Salette.

He had seen death approaching, and with it the dazzling Virgin who had chosen him for herself at a very tender age and whom he now longed to see face to face and love forever in eternity.

"In giving their narrative of the Apparition, the shepherds had said: 'If we only had known that it was a great saint, we would have asked her to take us along with her!' On quoting these words the zealous Missionary cried out as though in ecstasy: 'More fortunate indeed are we than the shepherds, dear Mother; we know who you are and we do not hesitate to say: 'trahe nos post te (draw us after you)'; — I know that our portion here below is to weep ever our sins; we despise them! Ours is to raise our eyes to heaven; our one ambition is to possess it! . . . Our hearts long for you, O Mary! May we one day see you in heaven above! Your wonderful Apparition here on earth is but a glimpse of the glory which is yours in heaven ... On to heaven then ... On to heaven!" (25)

On the very day of Fr. Berthier's death, the Rev. Rector of the Holy Family School whom the Founder had chosen as his successor, wrote as follows to Fr. Perrin, Superior General of she Missionaries of La Salette:

> "It grieves us very much to announce the death of our dear Father and Founder, Fr. Berthier, whom God called to his reward on the 16th of this month. He had been suffering from a cold for several weeks; this was not serious enough to confine him to bed or force him to interrupt his customary duties.

On the morning of the 16th, as he was preparing to say Mass, he was seized with a sudden indisposition; his cold must have affected his heart; his condition was so weak that we felt the end was not far off. After receiving Extreme Unction, he fell asleep peacefully in the Lord after only a few minutes agony; he was conscious to the very end. His children, the Missionaries of The Holy Family, recommend him to your kind prayers and those of your Congregation. He will be buried in the community cemetery where his remains will lie alongside those of Father Pons, his helper and confrere of La Salette." (26)

Perfect Fidelity to His Vocation

Fr Berthier's life may be characterized as one of great missionary activity and of deep love of Our Lady of La Salette. His apostolic influence lives on even though he is dead and his love of Our Lady of La Salette continues to be felt everywhere. His tomb in a faraway land bears witness to and is a proof of, the perfect fulfillment of his missionary vocation.

On this side of that tomb, the numerous works which he composed and the flourishing Institute which he founded continue to propagate his Salettine apostolate throughout the world.

He wrote the following in his brochure on "late vocations": We have written for priests, for religious for Christian virgins, fathers and mothers and for young children, collecting for each group what we thought would he able to do them the most good. Now that this long and laborious work has come to an end, we have it much at heart to see it fulfill the purpose he had in mind when we undertook it and we desire very much that it continue, even after our death, to provide Christian souls with solid doctrine and practical advice. We will be very grateful to "those who will cooperate with us in attaining these objectives." (27)

Cardinal Langenieux thanked him for sending him a copy of the brochure and predicted that his work would be successful and would continue to effect good long after he was gone.

The Cardinal wrote from Reims on November 21, 1901, and said: "I thank you very much for dedicating your recent little book to me. You know that I am most interested in this work of yours which at its very inception received the blessing and encouragement of the Holy Father. I wish to again to express my interest in, and my happiness over, the progress that has been made up to now and the fine cooperation which you have received."

"The appeal which you are making will he answered by generous souls who have at heart the glory of God and the salvation of souls. You make it so easy and advantageous for them to help you. I am referring to a wide spread circulation of your many books which are all very well known and universally appreciated. Persons is the world, religious men and women and the clergy may well use them for their own instruction and assist in spreading them because of the great good these books could do; another reason for them to help in a wider propagation of your books is that the revenue accruing from the sales thereof contributes to the education and training of your future missionaries." **(28)**

These 'future missionaries', the present-day members of the Holy Family Community, are carrying on efficaciously the wonderful work of their saintly Founder. As do the Missionaries of La Salette to whom they are united by the closest of family ties, they labor to make Our Lady of La Salette known and loved; if need be, they are ready to defend the Apparition. The Missionaries of Our Lady of La Salette make Mary's teaching known to Christians in many countries throughout the world; likewise also do the Missionaries of the Holy Family carry on the same Marian and Salettine ministry in the many countries of Europe, America and Asia.

Thus it is that the spiritual sons of Fr. Berthier and those of Fr. Archier, Fr. Giraud and Fr. Perrin unite and cooperate as brothers in seeing to it that Mary's Apostolic Message of September 19, 1846, be made known throughout the world as she requested and made clear in her twice-repeated command to the little shepherds of the mountain: *Well, my children, you will make this known to all my people.*

Endnotes

(1) *The Wonders of La Salette* (1898), p. 339; (2) Ibidem, p. 341; (3) *The Work*, etc. (1902), p. 10; (4) Rule 12. – De Lombaerde, cited above, p. 518; (5) Letter from Miss D. L., reconstituted and written by Mâcon in April 1909, kept in the Archives of the Missionaries of La Salette; (6) De Lombaerde, cited above, p. 414; (7) Letter preserved in the Archives of the Institute of the Holy Family in Grave (Holland). – De Lombaerde, cited above, p. 388; (8) Same archives; (9) Letter kept in the same archives; (10) Ibidem; (11) Letter kept in the same archives. She is quoted by De Lombaerde, cited above, p. 389; (12) Register of decisions of the General Council of the Missionaries of La Salette and Archives of the Institute of the Holy Family; (13) From a "Copy of Letters", 4th volume, p. 398-399, Reims, home of Fr. Compant, Vicar General. Recorded and communicated by Fr. Ramers; (14) Archives. Circular no. 1; (15) Archives of the Institute. Circular no. 20, p. 5; (16) De Lombaerde, cited above, p. 519; (17) De Lombaerde, cited above, p. 454. – *Notes by Fr. Patarin*: "When I arrived at the mission of the Holy Family, the students were not numerous, maybe ten, twelve at the most; at least four of them became priests, including the immediate successor of Fr. Berthier as Superior General. I was the auxiliary of Father in the month of August 1898 in the first days from April 1901, for about two years and eight months." — Fr. Pons came to Grave some time before my departure, writes Patarin again. Recalled to France, I was first placed at the residence in Grenoble, rue Joseph-Chanrion to prepare myself for the ministry of preaching.

At the time of our exodus in October 1901, I had to accompany the dear Apostolic School to Tournai where I exercised the functions of supervisor until 1905."; (18) De Lombaerde, cited above, p. 474; (19) Ibidem, p. 475; (20) Written letter of Tournai – in February 1909; (21) De Lombaerde, cited above, p. 518; (22) Ibidem, cited above, p. 563; (23) De Lombaerde, cited above, p. 566; (24) Ibidem, p. 515; (25) Ibidem, p. 518; (26) Letter from Fr. J Carl, kept in the Archives of the Missionaries of La Salette; (27) *The Work of the Holy Family* (1902), p. 56; (28) Letter written from Reims, Nov. 21, 1901, kept in the Archives of the Holy Family.

La Salette and Holy Family members gather for blessing of the new Fr. Jean Berthier Chapel (left) on the Holy Mountain of La Salette.

Epilog

With the passage of time after the initial publication of this book in French about the life and ministry of Fr. Jean Berthier, M.S. by Fr. Victor Hostachy, M.S. in 1943 as well as its translation into English by Fr. Joseph Boutin, M.S., in 1953, we are finally publishing this book for the English-speaking world and making it available online in paper and e-Book versions. This is also time to update the results of the life and ministry of Fr. Jean Berthier, M.S.

First, his mission to make the La Salette message known has left us with an astounding commitment to educate and has enlightened God's people about the tenets of our Catholic faith through his extensive writings.

Second, his life's legacy includes the marvelous gift to the Church of the worldwide religious communities of the Missionaries of the Holy Family and his own membership in the La Salette Missionaries. Their contributions to the life of the Church are immeasurable and live on in the ministry and charism of these vibrant religious communities.

Third, a decision was made to transfer the body of Fr. Berthier to a most appropriate site – a new small chapel on the Holy Mountain of La Salette in France – with the countless visitors to La Salette throughout the years to come, asking for his intercession as a revered devotee of Our Lady of La Salette.

And, finally, on May 21, 2018, the Congregation for the Causes of Saints promulgated the decree on the heroic virtues of the Founder of the Missionaries of the Holy Family, the Venerable Fr. Jean Berthier, M.S. This resulted from his truly extraordinary life, ministry and dedication. All this has been possible through the grace of God and belief in Fr. Berthier's powerful intercession.

May the message of Our Lady of La Salette continue to be a gift to all God's people and offer reconciliation and healing, continuing to build the kingdom of her Son until he comes again.

Fr. Ron Gagne, M.S., editor

www.ingramcontent.com/pod-product-compliance
Lightning Source LLC
LaVergne TN
LVHW051838080426
835512LV00018B/2945